HAPPY TO HELP

A Mother's Biography Of

Aaron Jeffers

Written By

Joy M Lescott

"Kwayme, your extremely talented and musically creative brother wrote you a moving rap/trap beat – all about the lovely you. I am so very proud of him for how he is coping with the loss of you. He is so incredibly strong, sensitive, empathetic, caring, loving, affectionate and awesome just like you. Lots of love Mom xx"

Why'd You Have To Go?

"Like why'd you have to go,
Like why'd you have to leave,
Now I'm left with all this stress, it feels like I can't breathe
And it feels like you're still here but I know that you're not,
This song is for my bro, I miss you a lot (x2).

We have so many memories that I'll not forget.
You helped me with my problems, taught me manners and respect.
When I found out you were gone,
My life was a mess, and now you're up in heaven, I wish you the best.
I know that you're proud of the person I've become,
I've made some bad decisions but so does everyone.
You were always there for me when I needed support,
Man it's such a shame that your life had to end so short.

Please tell me why you had to leave my life,
Sometimes I break down and cry, reminiscing about those times.

Like why'd you have to go,
Like why'd you have to leave,

Now I'm left with all this stress, it feels like I can't breathe
And it feels like you're still here but I know that you're not,
This song is for my bro, I miss you a lot (x2).
On the day that you passed,
I broke down in tears.
Your life had gone so fast, my mind was full of fear.
Like what would I do, how would I live without my bro,
Like where should I go, I didn't know,
I really didn't know.
You were a very important part of my life,
And now in my head I'm just thinking why'd you have to die,
Sometimes I wish that I could just spread my wings and fly,
Up to heaven so that I could say my last goodbye.

Please tell me why'd you had to leave my life,
Sometimes I break down and cry, reminiscing about those times.

Like why'd you have to go,
Like why'd you have to leave,
Now I'm left with all this stress, it feels like I can't breathe
And it feels like you're still here but I know that you're not,
This song is for my bro, I miss you a lot" (x2).

Song written by K.Dubz (aka Bro), aged 13

CONTENTS

DEDICATION i

ACKNOWLEDGMENTS v

Who Was Aaron Silas Cephas Jeffers 1

Meaning, Origin & History Of The Name Aaron – Behind The Name 2

Education 45

Night Life 62

Birmingham Metropolitan College – James Watt Campus 65

Sporting Achievements 68

Blossoming College Friendships 79

Career 2009 – 2013 Retail Success 82

ASDA Colleagues' Statements 90

Personal Life 92

Last Birthday Celebration 99

The Day My Son Died 102

Wishes For My Grandson 117

Eternal Love: Mother's Love 120

Funeral Of Aaron Jeffers 126

Dealing With Grief After The Funeral 175

Dealing With Your Grief 193

How Writing Can Help Grief & How It Can Help You 214

Healing Questions To Ask Yourself When Mourning 225

ABOUT THE AUTHOR 236

DEDICATION

Legacy. A word we often associate with public figures - professional athletes, movie stars. People who do big things on big scales. But how do we define it when we are talking about an everyday person? Someone who was in the spotlight, yet the mark they made on other people's lives was significant in their own right?

Thinking about it and replaying it in my mind, I have so much love for your life Aaron, for the joy you gave to me and others, for the experiences you had. Legacy does not mean money or fame. Legacy is all about the mark we make on another person's life. It is about the love we spread and the kindness we share.

I interacted with a number of people who contributed to, and helped me to write this book. Each and every one of them told me how fortunate THEY were to have known you. While the grieving process will continue, I will be forever grateful to have been your mother and to know unconditional love - THAT is a legacy.

Please forgive me for not spending as much time with you at your resting place as I would, we both would, have liked. I had to figure out WHY and articulate my own unique divine purpose for writing this book about you from conception as an idea that sprung to mind during a conversation that was presented to me by a family member, Heather in 2018. I needed to get the clarity, motivation, confidence and focus to write and publish this book in 2020. I actually got so choked up and tearful, I had to walk away from the laptop and compose myself numerous times, so you can imagine how I felt when I got to your death scene. Not only was it heart-wrenching to write about you, I also found it daunting to type the final panels of an iconic character such as you, loved and remembered by millions of people of all ages – it felt like craving for something so bad, knowing that you cannot have it. I had to devote and schedule time to sit down and type, collate all of the essential information, not forgetting proof-reading this written material to be better prepared for the writing process ahead in between working full-time, raising your younger brother, Kwayme (now 15 years old) maintaining our home, plus finding time for personal time and growth. Setting an end date for writing this book forced me to stay on schedule and keep the forward momentum going to get my mind in gear, ready to produce this valuable piece of work. On the other side of the coin, it has been extremely exhilarating, amusing, exciting and rewarding writing this book. I have loved every second of the research work involved and information gathering. I still cannot believe to this day I am writing my own book – finally I have found closure.

I dedicate this book to you Aaron, my darling, my sweetheart, my amazing and remarkable first-born. You were one-of-a-kind! Your shining smile, your adorable laugh, your endless energy: there was no one like you in the whole world! Whenever you need a reminder of how amazing you are, just open this book and remember that we all love you always and forever. I love you more than words can say. Near or far, you are always on my mind and in my heart because you make the world a brighter place by just being you. I am so proud and honoured to be a mother to 2 awesome human beings.

PS: I have arranged in this book a display of your photographs from birth until adulthood. You would have disliked that, but I wanted to showcase you. I wanted everyone to see what a fantastic son you have been over the years.

Sending all my love, kisses and affectionate hugs your way!

Mother xx

*

I would also like to dedicate this book to my beloved grandson. I will be concealing your real identity to protect and respect your privacy. I wrote this book with you in mind, and especially for you.

I just wanted to leave you with this wonderful and precious legacy book as a treasured possession for you to keep close to your heart in memory of your astounding father.

I pray that creating and sharing this book of memories with you about how great your wonderful and inspirational father was, gives you a special gift of him from me.

This book will give you the opportunity to share stories about your daddy's life; about his childhood and teenage experiences and how he lived. These stories will also let you know who he was and how much he was loved by so many people. These stories will create a sense of history and heritage for you. Even if you do not fully appreciate these stories now, it is very likely you will later in life, and thus will create that legacy of memories in the hope that you will live on in your father's footsteps.

So, I pass on your father's most important and enduring legacy — his wisdom, lessons, hopes and dreams. It will give you permission to cry and miss him, however I know your daddy would want you to go on and live as fully as you can, knowing he will always be right here with you, as close as this book.

I know your father is not present in your life today, but he is in your life in spirit. At least Uncle Kwayme, I and the rest of the Lescott family have you in our heart, and that means a lot to us. Your father left a precious gift behind – you, for me and my family to cherish. We are so fortunate to have you in our lives and it gives us an enormous amount of comfort to hear your voice and see you through your father.

According to your mother, it was your father's greatest wish should he have lived to guarantee Uncle Kwayme and I were a part of your life. It was your great grandmother, Elise Lescott that shared with me how much your daddy wanted Uncle Kwayme to ensure that you were deeply loved just as much as your sister, but he never got the chance to fully articulate that to Uncle Kwayme in person. So, now you know just how much your father was forward thinking and planning for the future; how much he loved and cared about you even before you were born.

I would like you to know and fully understand grandson that sometimes things happen throughout the course of our lives that we simply have no control over. Whether it is a serious illness, or the loss of someone we deeply love, or losing something that means the world to us. There are also things that happen in life that we can be solely responsible for: that we are ashamed of, and wish we could take back, but we cannot. All that stress, pain, and resentment can be a heavy burden on our shoulders. Even though we cannot change our past to make the present better, we can however make a change in ourselves to brighten our future.

Firstly, you must have faith and put the situation in Jehovah God's hands because he cares about you and truly let go, accept the situation that you are in. Secondly, you must be able to re-assure yourself that everything in life happens for a reason. Whatever burden(s) you are facing in your life is not accidental. Thirdly, you must simply look at the situation as an opportunity for a new beginning. Finally, you are still capable of doing great things in your life, but first you must accept your past and build on it. Just remember, it is all about accepting who you are, what the situation is, and how you can turn your situation around and make it into something magical and amazing, just like I have done in this book dedicated to you.

We hope you have enjoyed and had endless fun with all the birthday and Christmas gifts Uncle Kwayme and I have sent your way over the years, not forgetting all of the enjoyable times we spent together and all of the numerous phone call attempts Uncle Kwayme and I made to your mother, particularly on your 6th birthday during social distancing COVID 19 2020 lockdown to try and maintain the connection between us and your extended Lescott family. Our fondest hope is that the love of both Uncle Kwayme and I, and your extended family (Lescott's) will continue on for generations to come.

This is your Nanna Lescott letting the rest of the world know, too. My dear grandson, may this book be also dedicated to you.

Xxx.

ACKNOWLEDGMENTS

"Jehovah God, I thank you for giving me the strength to keep going when all I really wanted to do was give up during and after the traumatic loss of my first-born child, Aaron. I prayed for strength during this difficult time, and you provided. You were always here for me, to give me strength and lift my heart when all seemed so hopeless. I am truly grateful for everything you have done for me, and for everything you are about to do for me. I want to thank you Jehovah God most of all, because without you in my life, I have no purpose, and without purpose, my life has no meaning. Without meaning, my life has no significance or hope. Amen. xx

Most importantly for my second-born son Kwayme, I would like to thank you personally for your patience during my very long days, nights and weekends at the laptop to successfully complete this project. Thank you for your understanding; all of your creative ideas and contributions in assisting me to close out this venture which reaches to the depths of my soul from those gorgeous big brown eyes of yours. Thank you for the unconditional love you show me each and every day, with that perfect beaming smile when I steal those precious moments to just sit and be with you. I love you always and forever. Amen. xx

To my loving parents and stepmother: Elise, Jestina and Cephas Lescott thank you for being my champions throughout the past 54 years of my life. Your unconditional love and support have meant the world to me, I hope that I have made you proud. Without you, I would not be where I am today. I cannot begin to express my gratitude to my family – sisters: Indiana and Claudia, brothers: Colin and Junior, niece: Shanai and nephews: Simeon and Shakeel and cousins for all of the love, support, encouragement and prayers you have sent my way along this journey. I love each and every one of you forever. xx

I would like to extend my deepest gratitude to all of my friends and colleagues for providing me with useful insight and suggestions, encouragement and guidance behind the scenes throughout the duration of this mission. Thank you for believing in my work and in my abilities. xx

A special thanks to my London family – Heather, what an inspiration you are to me. You were the one who imbedded the concept of writing this book deep within my soul. Many thanks for coming up with the idea for the title of this book. A massive thank you again, for your amazingly creative talent – designing, printing, and timelessly delivering the boxes of order of service all the way from your home town to be with Aaron at his funeral – so beautifully crafted. Many thanks also to Pat, Ian, James, Sandra, Aaron, Daniella, Chelle, Lee, Robyn, Jackie, Azzie and Aunty Joy for your presence, messages, kind thoughts and continued support during and after Aaron's funeral. Love you all like cooked food. xx

Throughout the process of writing this book, and as mentioned previously many individuals from the local community have taken time out to help me finalise this book. I would like to give a special thanks to all of the ASDA Perry Barr, Birmingham community as a whole for allowing me to personally conduct interviews with you to gain insight into Aaron's relationships with you; his work colleagues and customers, as well as gather information about his achievements during the time he was employed at the ASDA Perry Barr Store. I have to say, that experience was very emotional for me and I am sure it must have been for you too. However, the whole experience left me feeling totally inspired, energised and enthused with clarity. Thank you all for actively taking part in researching and providing me with both verbal and written contributions for inclusion in this book.

A special thank you to the ASDA Perry Barr, Birmingham Crew, including (Management, Pearline R, Darrett S, Mavis S, Sharon K, Bal K, and Lena) to name a few, for kindly offering their time, hospitality and refreshments at Aaron's funeral and all of the wonderful gifts beautifully wrapped for my grandson, shortly after he was born. Not forgetting all of the ASDA shoppers who provided heartfelt donations and written condolence messages, some of which I have shared with you in the latter chapters of this book.

In honour of my teachers, I will not be revealing the identity of those involved as a way of protecting and respecting their privacy and that of their families – you know who you are. You were the ones who urged me to learn the true meaning of the words 'looked after,' and why children and young people in society become 'looked after.' You all trusted me with an enormous task and left an indelible impression. I am completely blown away and very proud of each and every one of you for your strength, character and the courage you have all had to completely turn your lives around today. I am extremely grateful to you, Gill Jones for trusting me with this rewarding opportunity – thank you for the wonderful experience. I will treasure it for a lifetime.

Desmond Jaddoo – thank you for all of the concern and support you showed to me and my family pertaining to Aaron's overall health and well-being. I would like to take this opportunity to thank you and your wife, Yvonne for kindly welcoming me into your home, and for the continued support you displayed to me and my family at such a very traumatic and painful time in our lives. Thank you for fighting with me to try and get to the bottom of Aaron's sudden passing. As a member of the local community, you voluntarily collaborated with medical professionals involved to investigate, try to achieve and deliver change. You took both individual action, as well as action with others in the community, in a planned way to bring about a clearly identified and agreed change, with the vision of contributing to an improvement in quality of life. May Jehovah God continue to bless you and your family.

Losing my dear son, Aaron was not easy and so it was so comforting for me and AJ's family to be able to pass all of the funeral arrangements on to Goodridge-Milford Funeral Directors. Many thanks Sharon for your professional, well structured, personalised, well controlled with clear direction and organised service. Everything from directing the funeral; floral tributes to cemetery administration were taken care of along with beautiful gifts that included the releasing of doves at Aaron's graveside. On behalf of my family and I, to you and your team, thank you once again. xx

Finally, I would like to thank Suzanne Dottin-Payne, Sarah Francis and Anthony Towey for their constructive criticism of this manuscript. Your feedback has been invaluable. Suzanne, I am glad this book provided you with some food for thought. I hope that I have inspired and encouraged you to begin writing your own book about your personal experiences, and I offer you my support as a way forward. Writing a book about the story of ones' grief journey is a surreal process. I am forever appreciative to Sarah Francis for her editorial help, keen insight and on-going support in bringing Aaron's story to life. Anthony, I am so sorry for making you cry when proof-reading this book. Your reaction to it confirms to me that what you read and digested touched your very soul. I am truly grateful to you as copy-editors, and will remember this for the rest of my life. xx

I thank all of the people who contributed to my success and who taught me the ropes. Your contribution to my success is noteworthy and invaluable.

A very special thanks to everyone who helped with publishing this book.

The following pages contain the honest, heartfelt and touching memoir I wrote about my son, Aaron (aged 23, 6 months) after he died.

Jeffers posing at ASDA Perry Barr, Birmingham in 2012

Born: Aaron Silas Cephas Jeffers
                 29 September 1990
                 Birmingham
Nicknames: 'Jeffers', 'AJ', 'Azza', 'AJizay', 'King AJ', 'Mimic', 'Tinch'
                 (Tinchy Stryder lookalike), 'The Man' and 'Bow Wow' (Shad
                 Gregory Moss lookalike).
Died: 13 March 2014
                 (Aged 23, 6 months)
                 Queen Elizabeth Hospital, Birmingham
Resting Place: Witton Cemetery, Birmingham
Education: Mansfield Green Community School, Birmingham (Primary)
                 George Dixon International School, Birmingham (Secondary)
                 Birmingham Metropolitan College – James Watt Campus,
                 Birmingham
                 Matthew Boulton College, Birmingham
Occupation: Store Colleague/Self Scan Host
Children: 1

Who Was Aaron Silas Cephas Jeffers

Infectious smile, handsome, well-mannered, inspiration. These words described Aaron perfectly.

Aaron Silas Cephas Jeffers (29 September 1990 – 13 March 2014) was an ASDA Store Colleague - Self Checkout Host and amateur footballer. Born in Birmingham, Jeffers participated in his school's Football Team and several local football matches from a young age.

Meaning, Origin & History of the Name Aaron – Behind The Name

When it came to naming Aaron, the historical reasoning behind his secondary names and his family name were in honour of both his grandfathers' first names. Jeffers' parents wanted to commemorate something precious to them.

The name Aaron is of Hebrew origin and means 'high mountain' and 'exalted'.

Biblically, Aaron was the courageous spokesman for his brother, Moses, when they appeared before Pharaoh. Moses was 3 years younger than his brother Aaron. Jehovah God later appointed Aaron to be Israel's first high priest.

Aaron's given word was as secure as the gold in Fort Knox. Honour and dignity was as necessary for him as air and water. Only with knowledge and respect could you become a part of this young man's life!

Born Day

On this day, 29th September 1990 and at that moment Joy, Aaron's mother was the happiest she had ever been in her entire life.

"This is the best day in my entire life," she told him.

The 29th September 1990 was a very special evening for Joy. It was the day her baby Aaron was born. He was born at The City Hospital, Dudley Road, Birmingham, and weighed 8lb 6oz.

Joy lay at a slight incline in bed as the contractions came and went with only lines on the monitor to make her aware of them. She resumed her wait for her son's arrival. Joy, soon mother-to-be paid attention to the facial expressions of the nurses. They communicated with each other. And just like that, the team of medical professionals came in and did their job.

After 18 hours slow labour, Joy finally heard her first born cry. She got to see him for the first time. There was nothing that could be compared to that feeling. It's a boy! — her beautiful and darling son, Aaron. Joy was already like a child with a new toy, very content and happy.

Aaron's grandmother, Elise could not hide her joy either when she saw her grandson. Relatives and friends were also happy to welcome the new arrival to the Lescott family, and organised colourful celebrations with family members and friends to share the joy of having a new arrival.

Aaron is featured below with Elise, a few hours after her daughter gave birth to him.

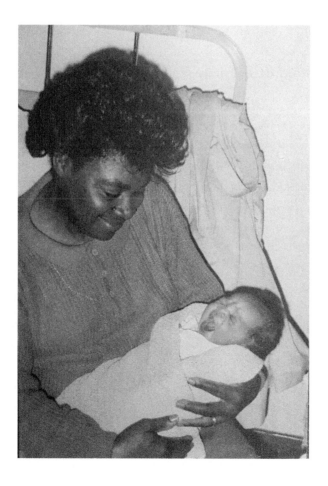

Elise commented:

"It was an absolute blessing to hold you on the day of your birth knowing that one day you would soon grow up into manhood. Unfortunately, when you were 23 years of age, you took ill and passed away.

We all love you dearly and will miss you always. It is a promised hope from the Almighty that I, your grandmother will see you again in Jehovah God's new world, where there will be no more pain, sickness, no more death and no more suffering in Jehovah God's new order.

It will be just peace and happiness. I hope I will be there to hold you once again, and welcome you back in paradise on earth. Here is what Psalms 127:3 says: "Look! sons are an inheritance from Jehovah God. The fruit of the womb is a reward."

Childhood & Teenage Years

Aaron is survived by his older brother Jerome, younger brother Kwayme (15) and younger sister, Zhane.

The avid footballer's mother, Joy, was the primary caregiver in his early childhood, and throughout his life.

The first physical and emotional relationship between both mother and son was established between the duo right after birth. Aaron depended on Joy for almost everything, and this secure attachment with his mother formed the foundation for a strong bond.

Mothers have a significant impact on their sons to the extent that the way they behave in their later years is attributed to their relationship with their mother. No other person understands a child better than a mother. Right from the time they are born till their adult years, a boy nurtures a deep-rooted bond with his mother, and their relationship is imperative for the overall development and emotional health of the child.

During early childhood, the bond between the pair began right inside the womb. Aaron picked up his first emotions from his mother and as the nurturing continued, he grew up to be emotionally intelligent and strong, learning to trust and feel emotional security.

Joy took a keen interest in Aaron's education, helping him to be good in his academics. Besides imparting education, she also helped him become emotionally adequate which is an absolute necessity for healthy living.

As a 4-year-old, Aaron used to cling to his mother at every possible chance; fast forward by 10 years he would not want his mom to enter his room. *"Son, you will outgrow my lap, but you will never outgrow my heart."*

Adolescence is a tough phase for boys where they may struggle to deal with a lot of changes internally and externally. Joy assisted Aaron get through the tough teenage years, succumbing to peer pressure. With open communication she openly explained the worldly ways to help Aaron differentiate between the good and bad. As an affectionate and empathetic mother, Joy provided stability and gave sound moral guidance to him.

In 2001 (aged 11), the lone parent discovered a short biography which Jeffers had written in one of his English lessons at George Dixon International School. He wrote:

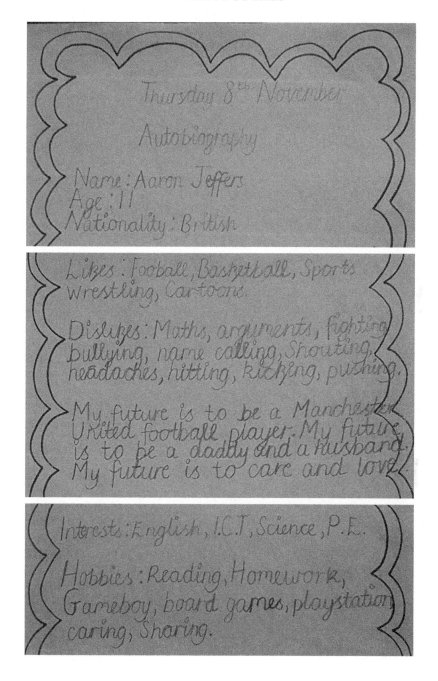

Teenagers like to be treated as adults. So, when Joy sought her son's inputs and suggestions in general or involved him in family discussions, he felt respected and it helped in increasing his self-esteem and confidence.

Adulthood

At the time of adulthood, that was the time when Joy counselled Aaron about his career, love and his future helping him stay focussed on his career and letting him be realistic in pursuing him to follow his passions and dreams.

She advised him: *"Respect others and respect will follow you. Do good and good will always follow you. Not everyone will admire your success. Not everyone will love you. You must know the value of good people in your life. Always listen to your heart when choosing friends."*

Learning To Drive & Driving Test

No matter how old you are, learning to drive can be an exciting and terrifying time. When we first learn to drive it can seem almost impossible, like we are never going to get the hang of it.

The excitement for Jeffers was learning a new skill that gave him a sense of freedom that he never had before. Driving opened up so many doors for him; it allowed him to go where he wanted, whenever he wanted to. Alongside his work in the retail industry, Jeffers pursued learning to drive. He no longer had to wait around or rely on other people anymore; it meant no more waiting at the bus stop in the freezing cold weather.

Aaron carried his love for driving into his driving lessons accompanied with his mother as a provisional driver in 2012. What began as learner driving continued as an act of determination. He had a fierce desire to prove to himself and others that he was competent and skilled to become a qualified driver. After a first few lessons, Jeffers eventually progressed onto right-hand turns and putting the car in 4th gear. The key skill with driving that Aaron mastered was having patience to do things gradually, and after a while it all eventually came to him.

Joy recalls Aaron stalling the car so many times at the red lights on the junction of Dyas Road & Kingstanding Road, Birmingham when practicing and improving hill starts without the handbrake being applied, to enable him to control the car at low speeds, making manoeuvres such as reverse parking much easier. One of AJ's challenges was to master and learn the art of clutch control. The first step of getting to grips with clutch control was finding and understanding his bite point. Joy remembers Aaron re-iterating several times to her *"I can't do it."* Despite these competitive situations, Aaron never gave up. Finally, he got the hang of it and clutch control became second nature to him.

On 29 February 2012, and after 3 attempts, Jeffers proved to himself, his family and friends that he was worthy as a professional driver. He passed his driving test at the Kingstanding Driving Test Centre, Birmingham and became a legal driver.

As a result of his sheer grit and determination, Joy treated the first-time driver to a car of his choice for his 21st birthday – Vauxhall Corsa SXi, petrol blue in colour. Jeffers named his ride 'Blue-Green' - his 'pride and joy.'

I am sure there is not a single driver in this country that has not felt it. The feeling of pure freedom when you get behind the wheel and turn the engine on. This again is a feeling that Jeffers experienced during his very first driving lesson – that moment when he felt relieved that nobody at work would see Joy dropping him off anymore. Yes, the love of driving ignited for him right there and then.

Those last 2 attempts before actually passing his driving test was when Jeffers so desperately wanted to be free of everything. Driving gave it to him. The moment he received his license was the start of a whole new beginning. It was the first moment of self-accomplishment, the success that unlocked an endless number of possibilities and routes ahead.

After all adrenaline is a huge part of the driving experience. Then there is the excitement of going places – the ability to drive away across cities or simply take a road trip. Jeffers felt like an explorer, and driving gave him a special vibe that made him feel part of nature, part of the world as he so much loved the outdoors.

When AJ was driving his Vauxhall Corsa from point A to point B, he felt in control of the world ahead of him, and his loved ones got to share that feeling with him, when they were on calm and enriching bonding adventures together. He would also make himself useful and pick up groceries for himself and his family or collect his younger brother from after-school club. Aaron always loved helping people, and one of the ways he did this was through driving.

Driving with other people gave Jeffers a chance to talk to them. He always enjoyed the conversations and laughter he had with people in his car, because they were almost guaranteed to last a while and he learnt what was on their minds, or he could talk about something that had been on his mind.

Aaron took a lot of pride in is driving, and always adhered to the speed limit. Driving gave him a chance to do what he loved, and he wanted to make it last for as long as he could.

'Blue Green' was Aaron's own territory – it became an extension of his home. A place where he felt at ease, and where driving was very often the little time that he had only for himself. Jeffers would be rolling with the windows down, elbows out because this was his 'me time.'

Joy also recalls on 21 June 2013, 'Blue-Green' was off the road for a short period of time. Jeffers was devastated that he could not drive. He had already learnt the components of the Vauxhall Corsa quite some time ahead of the purchase itself. The affection was already there before the car was in his possession.

When Aaron initially set eyes on his first ever ride, he was overflowing with emotions – it was his foremost, it was a car; it was the prime car that he could drive all by himself. Eventually, he started to seek moments where he could have little one-to-one interactions with the vehicle on the drive. He developed a relationship and an attachment – even the maintenance that he had to do on his car became a positive emotion. The soul of 'Blue Green' hid in its sounds, its smell, its interior and design was a factor for Jeffers.

Driving brought Aaron so much pleasure and happiness. He enjoyed his leisure motoring to the full and spent hours on end washing, cleaning and polishing his ride. Joy wanted him to continue to be mobile, so provided him with financial support to place 'blue green' back on the road.

To show appreciation, Jeffers wrote a brief note addressed to his mother to thank her for the support she offered at a time when she had gone through redundancy with her former employer, to which she dedicated 27 years of her working life:

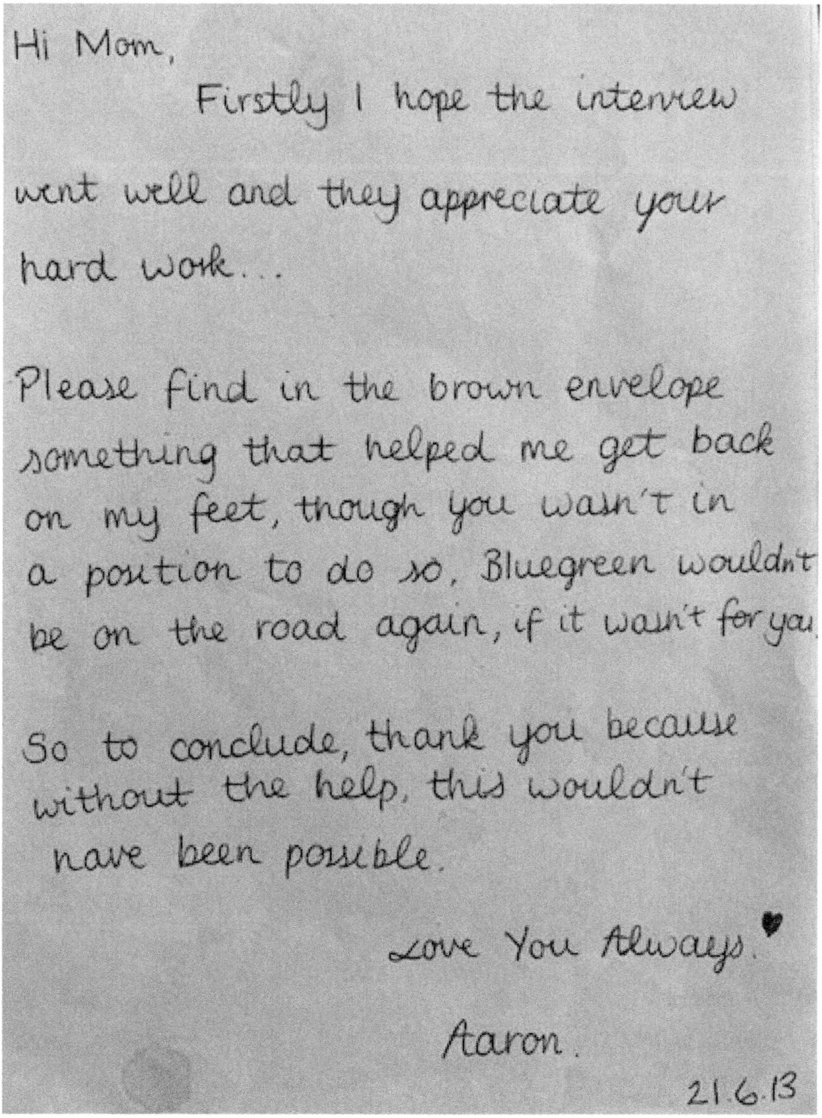

Hi Mom,

Firstly I hope the interview went well and they appreciate your hard work...

Please find in the brown envelope something that helped me get back on my feet, though you wasn't in a position to do so, Bluegreen wouldn't be on the road again, if it wasn't for you.

So to conclude, thank you because without the help, this wouldn't have been possible.

Love You Always ♥

Aaron.

21.6.13

As a responsible and professional driver, Aaron wanted his close friends and neighbours to possess the skills to be safe and responsible drivers for life when they received his coaching techniques – tools that helped him teach in a client-centred way. Client-centred learning is an approach to learning that takes into account how the learner prefers to learn.

When people learn in this way they are more likely to retain information and skills. People are also more likely to keep learning if they are encouraged to take responsibility for their learning at an early stage. At its simplest, this means listening to the learner to find out how they like to learn, the things that are getting in the way of their progress and how the coach can help.

Jeffers supported many of his close friends and neighbours (Daniel, Joel and Dominic) master their driving theory and driving test. He understood the theory test was an important part of learning to drive, and that it was vitally important to prepare for the theory test: learning about the rules of the road. Jeffers wanted the same for his friends and neighbours.

AJ loaned his Driving Test Success All Tests DVD to his next-door neighbour, Daniel in order for him to get used to what the multiple-choice test looked like on-screen, which his neighbour practiced on-line. The multiple-choice test covers topics such as alertness, road conditions and vehicle handling, incidents, accidents and emergencies. The questions in the multiple-choice test are taken from 3 books: The Official Highway Code, The Official DVSA Guide to Driving – The Essential Skills, Know Your Traffic Signs.

Jeffers also shared tips and various methods with his friends and neighbours that they could use to help them learn what they needed to know to get them through the driving test. He also provided guidance and asked hazard perception questions so that his neighbours and friends got the most out of their preparation, by checking they could recognise and respond to hazards that could happen while they were driving, and spot the developing hazards in each film on the DVD: probing for answers in terms of what his friends and neighbours would do as a driver, to take some action such as changing speed or direction. For example, a car pulling in to the side of the road ahead of them is a developing hazard because they would need to slow down and manoeuvre around it. What had seemed impossible for his friends, Aaron made possible.

Daniel wrote:

"I met Aaron when I was 11 years old. I moved in next door to Aaron and his family with Suzanne, my mother, a few months before Aaron and his family did. I remember seeing him out and about. I did not want to get involved or talk with him because I thought he was a gangster by the way he was dressed: snapback hat, jeans, Converse trainers, hoody and bomber jacket.

Putting my feelings aside, Aaron began to take an interest in my car. I am a classic car enthusiast and he also loved cars. I now own a classic car at the age of 23 and enjoy restoring and modifying a variety of classic vehicles as a hobby.

I invited him into my home and shared my model car collection with him, which I have accumulated over the years.

To help me successfully achieve passing my driving test, Aaron invited me in to his family home. We used to sit together and play music – we both naturally enjoyed the same types of music. Aaron encouraged me to book my theory test at my local driving test centre. He advised me to take some time out to revise using his Driving Theory Test DVD, which he kindly lent me.

I found the Driving Theory DVD very useful because it was packed full of useful tips and example questions related to multiple-choice questions and the hazard perception test made up of a series of video clips featuring a variety of driving hazards, like real life situations. I was able to test myself on-line and practice, replicating the conditions that I faced in the proper exam. Aaron would often test me to see whether I had been revising.

Keeping my car neat and tidy is a priority to me, and it was for Aaron too. When you mix adults with water, you usually end up with a fun time. Add to that some turtle wax, sponges and dirty cars, and you have tons of water fun and soaking wet clothes after all the jet-wash fights we used to share. We both set up car washes regularly, needless to say, hours of fun ensued."

Raising Music Lovers

Jeffers was always exposed to varied styles of music through his parents as a young child. His father is a DJ and began DJing from a young age. Aaron would listen to all types of music, in particular reggae, R&B, hip hop, rap and dance albums to expand his horizons and help him develop his own taste. Eventually he began to show interest in music.

AJ taught himself to dance at a young age and was inspired by musical artists such as Nat King Cole, Michael Jackson, Louis Armstrong, James Brown, Usher, Tinchy Stryder and Twister. He showed off his dance prowess by mimicking the dance moves of another one of his idols, Chris Brown.

His younger brother Kwayme, also a music lover can also be found listening to or playing music to elevate his listening experience; teach him something new about music, or allow him to experience his favourite music. In his spare time, the young Beat Producer composes and crafts original music, then mixes his own sampled material with original content, over rap and hip-hop artists lyrics.

Wrestling

WWE, the professional wrestling television programme produced by the World Wrestling Entertainment was one of Jeffers' favourite TV programmes, and he watched many wrestling videos as a teenager with this family and friends.

He enjoyed collecting the latest and greatest WWE wrestling figures, rings, championship belts, ring play sets, themed microphones and much more. He battled it out in authentic scale WWE arenas and recreated iconic matches with WWE heroes like:

Stone Cold Steve Austin

Proudly raising his middle fingers in the faces of everyone who dared oppose him, 'Stone Cold' Steve Austin was the blue-collar warrior. Clad in jeans and black leather often soaked in beer foam, Austin was defiant, brash and dared anyone to try and tell him what to do. When the signature sound of shattering glass erupted throughout the arena, everyone there knew that it was time to raise hell. And if you happened to be on the receiving end, well, you have our sympathies.

The Rock

With one eyebrow cocked, The Rock would warn jabronis to *"Know your role and shut your mouth"* or *"Just bring it!"* before delivering his devastating finishing manoeuvres.

Hulk Hogan

Hulk Hogan was one of the most beloved figures in the World Wrestling Federation in the 1980s, known for his flamboyance and the frenzy of his fans, which was referred to as 'Hulk mania.'

John Cena

Cena's long-time catchphrase is *"You can't see me."*

The Undertaker

The one thing and only thing that cements The Undertaker's legacy is THE STREAK. The Undertaker is famous for his wrestling persona which is made up of many different eras: The Deadman with the fedora hat and the trench coat with the tie around his neck; The Lord of Darkness; The Ministry of Darkness and The American Badass.

Shawn Michaels

Best known as the 'Heartbreak Kid.' He is also known as the man who made the ladder match popular.

Rikishi

Known for his bleached blonde hair, hip sunglasses and sumo wrestling gear. The big man formed a wildly popular alliance with the duo known as 'Too Cool', 'Grand Master Sexay' and 'Scotty 2 Hotty'. This trio was loved for their hip hop dance moves and for Rikishi's infamous signature manoeuvre — the 'Stink Face'.

Disney Films

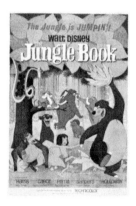

The Jungle Book (1967)

Since releasing the first full-length animated movie in 1937 (Snow White & The Seven Dwarfs), the name 'Disney' has become synonymous with excellent family entertainment. Jeffers picked the best of the best ever Disney movies for him and his family to enjoy. He would sit for hours on end watching, fast-forwarding and rewinding his favourite Disney animated movies.

Best Quote: *"I'm the king of the swingers, The Jungle VIP, I've reached the top and had to stop and that's what's botherin' me."*

Defining Moment: King Louie of the Apes and Baloo the Bear's scat-'n'-dance routine.

Jeffers' most lovable characters in this movie was Baloo and smooth-as-silk Shere Khan the Tiger. Singing along to Disney's musical numbers— 'Bare Necessities' and 'I Wanna Be Like You' gave Jeffers pure joy.

The Little Mermaid (1989)

The big song in the 1989 Disney film *The Little Mermaid* performed by Sebastian the Jamaican crab, trying to convince Ariel the mermaid that instead of joining the human world, she should enjoy the wonder life they lead underwater. The song is done in a Calypso style typical of the Caribbean, as the undersea creatures are, after all, tropical. Jeffers played the tune and was really absorbed. He loved it so much that he would dance and listen again and again.

Gaming

A massive fan favourite of Aaron's was Batman – his childhood hero. Batman displays sheer determination in the face of despair that makes him the brave and dynamic character we all love. Batman never gives in or gives up, he only gives it his all. Here are some snippets of what made Batman Aaron's ideal hero.

The Symbol

Batman's logo - undoubtedly the most recognisable icon that comes to mind not only in comics, but around the world. There is no chance of the black and yellow ever going unnoticed.

The greatest calling card there, the bat-signal allows Gotham's Dark Knight to clock in in times of distress. While Batman's preoccupied in the latest enquiry, he needs a way to act upon crises within moments.

The Bat-Mobile

The most popular and iconic means of transportation for Batman is the Bat-mobile - Batman's baby that he drives to be at the ready when disaster strikes. This alluring machine got Aaron daydreaming about how cool it would be to drive in it, let alone have it himself.

The Bat Cave

Its existence is kept hush, hidden underground through miles of potholes, and the convenience of it all right under the foundation of the Wayne establishment. Batman is not Batman without a bat cave, and he puts it to good use.

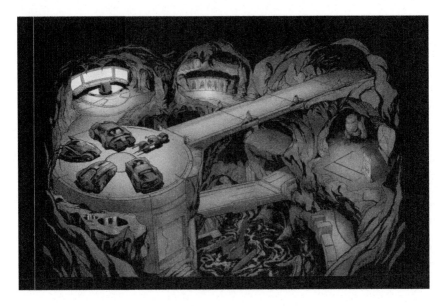

Jeffers loved playing Nintendo DS, Xbox 360 and PlayStation with his family and friends in order to connect with other gamers. Connecting for Jeffers was fun, as he could attend and host parties, invite his family and friends to play, chat, message, send friend requests and much more after a hard day's work. Jeffers' gaming and college homie, Paul, became a professional boxer, and he would get nothing but pure jokes all day long from playing Xbox and PlayStation together with Aaron.

On 12 November 2012 Jeffers wrote on Paul's (his boxer buddy's) Facebook page:

"Big Bro! Long-time man! Congrats on becoming champ, you deserve it. Proud of you. Even though I would knock you out 1ˢᵗ round LOL. Take care Azza."

There were certain songs Jeffers used to sing along to and put his own little twist on it whilst connecting with others on the Xbox 360. Jeffers' cousin, Shanai wrote on her Facebook page on 6 May 2014 (2 months after Jeffers passed away):

"So, I wanted to hear my cousin's voice and I remembered that my brothers Simeon, Shakeel and his friends made this video that Aaron is in. He is the guy at the start that is singing (as usual) and arguing with my brothers 2 minutes in. I did not cry, I laughed because this is a part of Aaron that I remember for those

of you who would like to hear his voice. I played it over and over. It was nice to hear his voice again. Reminded me of all the fun times we used to have on the Xbox."

Joy added: *"I too used to remember hearing many of the mini banter, singing, and endless laughter Aaron used to have during Xbox challenges with his cousins Simeon, Shakeel, Shanai and close friends. It was great – a reminder and emotional to hear Aaron's voice and laugh again. I played it over and over just like Aaron used to rewind his favourite moments to music, films and cartoons time and time again."*

On 26 November 2016, boxer pal Paul also wrote on Aaron's Facebook page:

"Playing Modern Warfare Remastered. I wanted the game not just because it is iconic, but it brings back memories of me playing with Aaron from back in college. I do not like to admit being second place anytime, but my brother was bad ass at this game. He made the other players in the game that angry to which he would simply reply "ha-ha" with his cheeky laugh (if you know you will know). Nothing but pure sarcasm. He made me laugh and when I remember he still does. Playing Xbox with Aaron was the funniest thing going. We both used to just mess around and tag team people. Good times. One of the fittest, smartest, politest and funniest person I will ever have the pleasure of meeting. Love you my brother."

Six months after Jeffers was laid to rest, on 28 September 2014 the fighter, Paul, dedicated his 4th professional boxing fight on his Facebook page to his *'dear best friend Aaron'*. The fight took place at the Hermitage Leisure Centre in Leicester. The support and turnout was brilliant, all for a good cause.

Paul, the professional boxer, comes from a fighting family who have been instrumental in the success of Nechells Amateur Boxing Club, Birmingham. He boxed out of the Nechells Green Amateur Boxing Club, which was founded by his great uncle. Paul has been around boxing all of his life and his father was a Class Amateur and former Midlands Featherweight Champion. The pro boxer had his first amateur fight at the age of 15 and turned pro in 2013.

In 15 years of boxing, Paul has never turned a fight down, boxed whoever was put in front of him, boxed all over the country and beat some good lads on the way.

'The Incredible', nickname comes from the pro's love of The Incredible Hulk, because he is strong and fights for the one thing he loves.

Movies

When Jeffers was in the mood for watching a movie or action-packed film at home to keep his mind whirling, he would check out very good movies filled with that extra kick to keep his attention.

Taken (2008) Bryan Mills (Liam Neeson), a former government operative, tries to reconnect with his daughter, Kim (Maggie Grace). Then his worst fears become real when sex slavers abduct Kim and her friend shortly after they arrive in Paris for vacation. With just four days until Kim will be auctioned off, Bryan calls on every skill he learned in black ops to rescue her.

The Expendables (2010) is a 2010 American action film written by David Callaham and Sylvester Stallone, and directed by Stallone, who also starred in the lead role. The film co-stars Jason Statham, Jet Li, Dolph Lundgren, Randy Couture, Terry Crews, Steve Austin and Mickey Rourke. A group of mercenaries is double-crossed during a mission and are approached by Church to overthrow the ruthless dictator of a South American country. It is not long before the men realise things are not quite as they appear, finding themselves caught in a dangerous web of betrayal. Although their mission is compromised and an innocent is in danger, soldier of fortune Barney and his comrades decide to get the job done.

Space Jam (1996) made shortly after Michael Jordan's first retirement from basketball and his short foray into professional baseball, SPACE JAM is a live-action/animation feature riding on the basketball superstar's coattails. Bugs, Porky, Tweety, and other favourite Looney Tune characters assemble a basketball team, including Michael Jordan as a member, to defeat a group of aliens, the Nerdlucks, who are trying to enslave the Tunes as attractions in their outer space theme park. The movie was a 1996 American live-action/animated sports comedy film directed by Joe Pytka. Starring basketball player Michael Jordan, the film depicts a fictionalised account of what happened between Jordan's initial retirement from the NBA in 1993 and his comeback in 1995, in which he is enlisted by the Looney Tunes to help them win a basketball match against a group of aliens who want to enslave them for their amusement park. *Space Jam* received mixed reviews from critics for its merits of combining Jordan and his profession with the Looney Tunes characters, while the live-action and animated mix especially the animated basketball scenes, Jordan's performance and faithful interpretations of the Looney Tunes were praised. The film was a box office success, opening at No. 1 in the North American box office and grossing over £230 million worldwide, becoming the highest-grossing basketball film of all time. *Space Jam* is full of familiar characters that earned Jeffers' trust and affection decades ago.

Like Mike – Kids cannot be Michael Jordan, but they can wear his basketball sneakers, and in their fantasies, the sneakers give them the power to be - like Mike. Lil' Bow Wow stars as Calvin Cambridge, an orphan who comes into possession of a pair of faded Nikes with the initials 'MJ' written inside the tongue. Calvin and his friends, who all live an in orphanage, find old shoes with the faded letters MJ connected to a power line. The 14-year-old, hoops-loving Calvin Cambridge has a dream to be a famous basketball player -- to mix it up among the NBA's greatest. But in a game dominated by giants with unparalleled athletic abilities, Calvin's diminutive stature and limited skills, make this a far-off fantasy. One stormy night, they go to get the shoes when Calvin and the shoes are struck by lightning. Calvin now has unbelievable basketball powers and has the chance to play for the NBA. After he laces up a mysterious pair of old sneakers inscribed with the faded initials MJ, Calvin makes the leap from playground hijinks to NBA superstardom.

As a young boy, Jeffers used to attend Arena Birmingham to watch a number of Basketball cup finals, which consisted of exhilarating days of hoops action and with line-ups featuring showpiece games. To add in to the mix was the incredible courtside fun and entertainment, days that lived in Jeffers' memory forever. The basketball lover loved the sport because it is fun to watch and brings out the best in the players. This is where the players give their all in the sport. The other reason as to why AJ loved basketball was because the sport is high paced. There is never a dull moment in the duration that the game is played.

Comedy

Comedy is a genre of film in which the main emphasis is on humour.

These films made Jeffers laugh through amusement, entertainment, and provoked enjoyment. Comedies provided Jeffers with merriment and a momentary escape from day-to-day life.

Giggle along to a few of the best comedy films, as voted for by Jeffers.

Barber Shop (2002) is an American comedy film directed by Tim Story, produced by State Street Pictures and released by Metro-Goldwyn-Mayer. Starring Ice Cube, Troy Garity, Cedric the Entertainer, and Anthony Anderson. Calvin (Ice Cube), who inherited the struggling business from his deceased father, views the shop as nothing but a burden and a waste of his time. After selling the shop to a local loan shark, Calvin slowly begins to see his father's vision and legacy and struggles with the notion that he just sold it out.

Next Friday (2000) is the first film to be produced by producer Ice Cube's film production company Cubevision. It was directed by Steve Carr and stars Ice Cube, Mike Epps, Don 'D.C.' Curry, John Witherspoon, and Tommy 'Tiny' Lister Jr. Craig (Ice Cube) bails his friend out of trouble, survives a climatic confrontation with Debo, the neighbourhood bully, and ends up with the girl. In *Next Friday* the bully is back as Debo, who spent two years behind bars, is released from prison. Fearing for his son's safety, Craig's father (John Witherspoon) sends his son to live with Uncle Elroy (Don "D.C." Curry). However, Craig soon

26

learns that trouble can find you no matter where you live.

House Party (1990) is a 1990 American comedy film released by New Line Cinema. It stars Kid and Play of the popular hip-hop duo Kid 'n Play, and also stars Paul Anthony, Bow-Legged Lou, and B-Fine from Full Force, and Robin Harris (who died of a heart attack nine days after House Party was released). The film also starred Martin Lawrence, Tisha Campbell, A.J. Johnson, Daryl 'Chill' Mitchell and Gene 'Groove' Allen (of Groove B. Chill), Kelly Jo Minter, John Witherspoon, with a cameo by funk musician George Clinton. Play's parents are out of town, and he is planning the house party to end all house parties. His best friend, Kid, wants to go more than anything, knowing Sydney (Tisha Campbell), the hottest girl in school, is sure to be there. But when Kid gets into a fight at school, his father (Kid 'N Play) grounds him. Still determined to go, Kid sneaks out of the house and faces one calamity after another as he makes his way to Play's house and the party of the school year.

**'Kenan & Kal'** is an American teen sitcom. The show originally aired on the Nickelodeon network for four seasons, from August 17, 1996 to May 3, 2000. Set in Chicago, Illinois, the series follows Kenan Rockmore and best friend Kel Kimble, who go on a number of misadventures. The show features Kenan's family, which consists of his father Roger, mother Sheryl, and younger sister Kyra. The show also features Kenan's boss Chris Potter. It won the 'Favourite TV Show' award at the 1998 Kids' Choice Awards. "Aw, here it goes!" is Kal's catchphrase.

Kenan Thompson and Kel Mitchell were among the original cast members of the popular Nickelodeon sketch-comedy series 'All That'

when they received their own sitcom in 1996. Set in Chicago, the show follows the kid-friendly misadventures of two high-school friends who are always scheming and dreaming.

Kenan, who works at a grocery store, constantly devises crazy plans to strike it rich, while orange-soda and ham loving buddy Kel is always dragged along for the ride despite his track record for messing things up. Kel is scared of pancakes, butterflies, brassieres, flying, Berlin and monkeys. Kel is quite clumsy, impulsive, naïve and accident-prone! Despite all this, Kel is quite intelligent, but just does not tend to show it! He is an incredible painter, an excellent violinist, a rapper and does very well in school, unlike Kenan.

Jeffers was a 90's kid and absolutely loved this show. He used to watch it when he was little, and he had so much fun laughing. Jeffers even copied the acting like he was Kenan or Kel. AJ was a huge fan of their shows because Kenan and Kel were the best dynamic duo, always scheming and plotting stuff and Kel just loved orange soda - they were so funny – WAY TOO FUNNY. THE BEST KIDS' COMEDY EVER and made Jeffers childhood literally.

'Sister, Sister' - is an American television sitcom starring identical twins Tia and Tamera Mowry. It premiered on April 1, 1994 and concluded after airing six seasons on May 23, 1999. The premise of the show was that the girls (playing characters Tia Landry and Tamera Campbell) were separated and adopted at birth. One was adopted by a single mother while the other was adopted by a couple, although the mother died a short time later. The two accidentally found each other fourteen years later and reunited. The twins are reunited during a chance encounter shopping at a clothing store at the mall with their adoptive parents.

Tia Landry is the intelligent twin from inner city Detroit, where her adoptive mother, Lisa, works as a seamstress Tamera Campbell is the boy-crazy twin from the suburbs, where her adoptive father, Ray owns a successful limousine service. After their unexpected encounter in the department store, Ray reluctantly allows Tia and Lisa to move into the house because Lisa was about to take a job in St. Louis, which would have separated the girls.

The girls' neighbour is nerdy Roger Evans (pictured below) an annoying teenager who is infatuated with both of them, and who evolves into a perfect gentleman they both find attractive.

In the final season when the girls go off to college, Roger ceases to appear in the series because he was still in high school, though he does return as a guest in the final episode. By the fifth season, Tia and Tamera ended up with steady boyfriends.

In the sixth-season episode 'Father's Day', the twins meet their biological father, and learn that he is white and a famous photojournalist. Their father never married their mother, because they never got the chance: she had been asked to paint a mural in Florida and he had been assigned "the opportunity of a lifetime" in the Middle East. Also, their mother told him that she would later join him in Tel Aviv without telling him of her pregnancy. After six months, their mother suddenly stopped writing. When the girls' mother died, their father was not allowed to see them because he could not prove he was their father. When he searched for his twin daughters, he never found them because they had been adopted by two different people.

Jeffers watched and laughed at the half-hour comedy series which chronicles the adventures of a reunited set of identical twins, in particular the hilarious, obnoxious and annoying Roger. His advances towards the twins were ill-received, and he usually tried to hit on the sisters while visiting them, at which point the sisters, including various members of the household would say the repeated chorus "Go home Roger!" after showing up uninvited; overstaying his welcome; being very annoying and childish.

"GO HOME ROGER" was one of the biggest catchphrases of 1990s TV shows, and saw poor Roger being banished from Tia and

Tamera's home in the hit show Sister, Sister.

Poor Roger never really got a look in with either of the girls, despite being madly in love with them.

This show was a staple feature of Jeffers' childhood. He used to watch this TV programme all the time when he was little too. It was funny, entertaining and was a great show for families to enjoy.

'Desmond's' - The tale of Peckham's most inept barber was Britain's most successful black sitcom. 'Desmond's' showed the lives of the Ambrose family, who all longed to improve their lot. Desmond, played by the late Beaton, dreams of retiring and returning to Guyana; Shirley, his wife, enrols in a French evening class in the opening episode; yuppy eldest son Michael aims to run the local bank; middle child Gloria wants to be a fashion writer; and youngest son Sean is on course to go to university. At its core, 'Desmond's' was a family show. It did not matter if you were black or brown or white, the story was for every family. It was not written solely for black people, it was for white people so they could see how black people really are.

At that time, the negative press about muggings and shootings was all black people seemed to get. 'Desmond's' ran for 71 episodes, ending in 1994 due to Desmond's health.

Like most great sitcoms, Jeffers looked forward to 'Desmond's' because it thrived on its running gags and side characters: the frequent jubilant cry "Yeah, mon" of Desmond's best friend Porkpie which he used to imitate weekly in order to entertain his family when these episodes used to come on.

Matthew, the perennial student from the Gambia with a penchant for "old African sayings" such as "the respectful goat doesn't fart in front of the chief"; and gossiping hypochondriac Beverley.

'Diff'rent Strokes' – an American sitcom that aired on NBC from 3rd November 1978 to 4th May 1985 and on ABC from 27th September 1985 to March 1986. The series starred Gary Coleman and Todd Bridges as Arnold and Willis Jackson as his older brother, two African American boys from Harlem who were taken in by a rich  white Park Avenue businessman and widower named Phillip Drummond, his daughter Kimberley (Dana Plato) and their maid who lived in a penthouse suite in New York City.

The two brothers were welcomed into the Drummond household and became part of the Drummond family, where they learned various lessons about life. The series made stars out of the child actors Gary Coleman, Todd Bridges and Dana Plato. The lives of these stars were later plagued by legal troubles and drug addiction with Plato and Coleman suffering early deaths.

Jeffers' mother remembers AJ watching the show when he was a teenager and the shows made him LOL. He kept watching the episodes randomly as an adult and they still made him LOL.

As Arnold, Coleman popularised the catchphrase "What'chu talkin' 'bout, Willis?" The first known use of this meme was in 1978.

Former child star, Gary Coleman, rose to fame as the wisecracking youngster Arnold Jackson, but grew up to grapple with a troubled adulthood, died at the age of 42.

'The Fresh Prince of Bel-Air' – is an American sitcom that originally aired on NBC from 10th September 1990 to 20th May 1996. The show stars Will Smith as a fictionalised version of himself, a street-smart teenager from West Philadelphia 'born and raised.' While playing street basketball, Will misses a shot and the ball hits a group of people, causing a confrontation that frightens his mother, who sends him to live with his wealthy uncle and aunt in their Bel Air mansion, Los Angeles.

In the series, Will's lifestyle often clashes with the lifestyle of the Banks family – Will's Uncle Phil and Aunt Vivian and their children, Will's cousins: Hilary, Carlton and Ashley. The series ran for 6 seasons and aired 148 episodes.

Although this was quite literally two decades ago, Jeffers knew the infamous lyrics and could not help but rap along to the theme song 'Yo home to Bel-Air!' The theme song was written by Will Smith and DJ Jazzy Jeff. These two, who literally played Will and Jazz in the show, were actually a hip-hop duo in the 1980s before the show was created and won a Grammy in 1989 for Best Rap Performance! Their most successful single was 'Summertime,' earning the group their second Grammy.

It only took 15 minutes to record and produced the theme song. Will and Jazz had 5 albums out by the time this show was in production. The song remained on the Top 40 Singles Chart for 10 weeks, peaking at number 3.

On 31st December 2013, Uncle Phil dies at the age of 68, from complications following open heart surgery at Glendale Memorial Medical Centre.

Smith portrayed Uncle Phil's nephew on the 1990's sitcom and paid tribute to his Fresh Prince of Bel Air co-star James Avery (Uncle Phil) by posting an updated photo of himself along with Avery and the rest of the cast on his Facebook page, writing that the picture was taken the last time they were together. Will wrote 'Some of my greatest lesson in acting, living and being a responsible human being came through James Avery. Every young man needs an Uncle Phil. Rest in Peace.'

It has been over 20 years since 'The Fresh Prince of Bel-Air' left NBC. Since then, Will has become a global brand, fighting aliens, vampires and Joe Frazier.

If you recall, Will and Carlton (Alfonso Ribeiro) reunited back in 2015 to rap the show's iconic theme song on the UK's 'Graham Norton Show'.

AJ was just addicted to this show. 'The Fresh Prince of Bel-Air' was a show that he never got tired of. Jeffers found Will Smith hilarious; everything he said always cracked him up. He loved the way

Will always picked on Carlton and Uncle Phil. There was also Geoffrey. Wow, he was the most sarcastic butler around and always made fun of Uncle Phil.

'The Cosby Show' - centred on the lives of the Huxtables: obstetrician Cliff and his lawyer wife Claire, their daughters Sondra, Denise, Vanessa and Rudy, and son Theo. Based on the stand-up comedy of Bill Cosby, the show focused on his observations of family life. Although based on comedy, the series also addressed some more serious topics, such as learning disabilities and teenage pregnancy.

What Jeffers loved the most about 'The Cosby Show' was that of the subject matter, and the lessons that the shows re-iterated the themes of self-respect and appreciation of others, whilst emphasising healthy romantic relationships. The show steered clear of any topics that might raise eyebrows, focusing mainly on the daily childrearing issues of a large family. With so many teens and preteens in the Huxtable house, many of the issues they faced related to boy/girl relations, and it was refreshing to see a household in which kids willingly brought their worries, concerns and frustrations to their parents' attention.

'The Cosby Show' also offered Jeffers subtly placed titbits of African-American history, music appreciation, and environmental awareness. 'The Cosby Show' was a classic family-friendly show that centred around an African-American family whose parents were educated professionals. Their parenting methods were gentle and trusting, and the kids responded with respect, with a clear realisation of what was expected of them.

'Everybody Hates Chris'

Everybody Hates Chris is a sitcom television series inspired by the childhood experiences of comedian Chris Rock, who narrated very hilarious and touching stories of a teenager growing up as the oldest of three children in Brooklyn, New York during the early 1980s.

A black teen in Brooklyn during the early 1980s attends a mostly white school in a sitcom 'inspired by the childhood experiences' of comedian Chris Rock. Bolstered by a soundtrack that beautifully  evokes the 1980s, the show chronicles the life of the young Chris, whose family's penny-pinching is leavened by love (and laughs). At home, Chris helps care for his younger brother and sister, while at school he is often the target of a racist bully. Chris' innate charm and sharp wit enables him to make new friends at school. Chris' parents work multiple jobs and still struggle to pay the bills, all while making sure their kids get a good education and stay on the straight and narrow.

This sitcom had Aaron laughing out loud in several spots throughout the seasons, and he looked forward to seeing more episodes of this show.

'My Wife & Kids'

 'My Wife & Kids' ran for five successful seasons between 2001 and 2005. Michael Kyle, a loving husband and modern-day man ruled his household with a unique and distinct parenting style on his quest for a 'traditional' family. Together with his wife Jay, son Junior and daughters Claire and Kady, Michael teaches his family some of the lessons of life delivered in his own unique brand of wisdom, discipline and humour.

The family members constantly gang up on each other before sharing advice and love at the end of the show. The jokes pulled are hilarious and funny, there is never really a dull moment with The Kyles and this is supported by its amazing and talented cast. The cast is fantastic and each one of them performs their role so well and with a large amount of confidence and manner. The show's environmental setting is basic but is suitable for the show's tone and the show's relationship between characters and people are amazing, there is a real strong sense of well bound chemistry between all characters and this just adds to the fact that this show is flawless and completely entertaining. The soundtrack for the show is nostalgic and laid back which is fantastic, My Wife & Kids was simply one of the best comedy TV Shows ever made and the non-stop quality of its 5 seasons prove and support that point.

Aaron found each and every episode of My Wife & Kids to be amazing, the story lines were interesting and ultimately entertaining. He thought the jokes pulled were hilarious and funny and there was never a dull moment with The Kyle Family.

Board Games

Monopoly - the Classic Edition of Monopoly! There is no better board game Jeffers could play with his friends and/or family when he wanted to spend hours finishing a game based around buying up real estate and being the 'winner' by earning the most money and making his associates bankrupt. What better way for Jeffers to spend a few hours barely keeping his rage in check when the person next to him landed on the one space he needed to complete a set of real estate?

Nothing brought Jeffers and his family together (or brought out their competitive side!) like a family board game. The family had timeless fun playing iconic family board games. In addition, Aaron and a group of his family members would often be huddled over the table leaping to their feet with a roar of jubilation.

Dominoes - hearing the slapping-down of domino tiles onto the table, and players leaping to their feet with a roar of excitement and laughter, as lines of tiles criss-crossed the table into the night, Jeffers soon learnt that Caribbean dominoes was a point of reference when islanders met each other for the first time.

A game of dominoes was far from quiet and peaceful. It was played very fast and a game was over in minutes. The dominoes were often slammed down hard for maximum effect and the atmosphere was sometimes tense.

Confident in their own abilities West Indians were keen to challenge anybody to a game, wherever they were. There is historical reason for the Caribbean's fanatical attachment to this game. Firstly, the game is played with passion and intensity. Secondly, players accompany the game with some form of drink, preferably rum. Thirdly, the game is played as loudly as possible, with high-decibel conversation and explosive slapping-down of the pieces onto the table.

Dominoes is without a doubt, a men's game and can be played with both the younger and older generation. Although you will rarely see women playing, that did not stop Jeffers from playing against his mother and other female players in his family, who were fierce competitors.

Xbox 360

Xbox 360 was the centre of Aaron's games and entertainment universe. He gamed with this console all the time with his cousins, college and work friends. AJ grabbed both new and pre-owned games for his Xbox 360. With a range of genres and awesome games to play with the Kinect, such as GTA; Olympic Games, Red Dead Redemption; Call Of Duty Black Ops; Call Of Duty Modern Warfare; Grand Theft Auto and Dance Central, using the Xbox 360 Controller to immerse himself in the best games the Xbox 360 had to offer. In addition, Jeffers used the Xbox 360 Kinect, which he found instantly fun - the Kinect got everyone off their seats and moving. The Kinect tracked his full body movement in 3-D giving precise and accurate reactions to each command and movement he made when he participated in all manner of activities with the Kinect, from playing sports to racing and much more. The whole family watched HD movies, TV shows, live events, music, sports and more and had hours of fun with this console.

Xbox One

Jeffers was extremely excited about the Xbox One, for the simple reason this console was the first run of Xbox One consoles, labelled as the Day One Edition that came with an exclusive Achievement and a Commemorative Controller, marked with the phrase "Day One 2013" right in the middle. A few days after its release (November 22, 2013), Aaron purchased the Xbox One entertainment system from his local GAME store in Perry Barr, Birmingham. Unfortunately, AJ never had the opportunity to play the next generation console, which was released after the Xbox 360. Jeffers was re-admitted into hospital in November 2013 and requested Joy to text him photos of the Xbox One console and games which he purchased before being admitted into hospital as a motivator - something to look forward to as his next destination home.

"Things in your bedroom are exactly how you left them. I visualise you on your Xbox. I will never be able to move your belongings — you are still part of the furniture. I have found all of your school books and wrestling figures you used to play with, not forgetting the collection of Converse trainers you owned. I am sure Kwayme will look after everything, as he has taken over your bedroom to be close to you. Kwayme says playing Xbox is not the same anymore. Hope you do not mind, but your cousins Simeon and Shakeel are wearing some of your Converse

trainers that you did not take out of the packaging. I hope when they wear them, they will look as fly as you did," wrote Joy.

Wii

With each passing year, video gaming became an exclusive experience. Nintendo created the most inviting, inclusive video game system, and thanks to this unique controller, Aaron, his family and friends played a variety of games on Wii – and they all had an incredibly fun time doing so.

Wii Party

Sharing the instant accessibility of titles like Wii Sports and Wii Fit, Wii Party brought more than 80 different mini-games into Jeffers' home. Here the Wii Remote became the star of the show, as the versatile Wii remote really came to life, making different animal noises for Jeffers, his family and friends to recognise. The remote would turn into a time bomb needing AJ to pass the remote to his neighbour as quickly as possible. The action transferred from the TV screen into the living room as they discovered a new way to play Wii. He also enjoyed playing pair games - the home of two-player action, and teaming up with another player, competing with them head to head.

Wii Mario & Sonic At The Olympic Games

Aaron competed in stylised Olympic venues with authentic sports and events to choose from when playing this game, including athletics, archery, skeet shooting, table tennis, gymnastics and more.

Jeffers would select his favourite playing style from the all-star cast of Mario and Sonic characters with four player types to choose from: all-around, technical, speed, and power.

For example: Mario (all-around), Peach (technical), Yoshi (speed), Bowser (power), Sonic (speed), Knuckles (power), Tails (technical), Amy (all-around). He would try out each event individually with single match mode, compete for the highest overall score in a series of events in circuit mode, or take on challenges created specifically for each character in the mission mode.

Wii Super Mario Bros

Aaron took on the adventures of Mario with his friends, where other players joined him at the same time on the same level at any time in the game to navigate the side-scrolling worlds of Mario for competitive and co-operative multiplayer fun. This game also introduced some fantastic new levels and surprises including quirky new suits, characters and innovative ways for Jeffers to use the Wii remote to guide his character through the adventure.

It was a lot of fun for Aaron to go back and play super Mario games. He was a big Super Mario fan and always played each game more than a couple times.

Wii Mario Kart

Jeffers' Nintendo Wii racing experience was enhanced when he utilised the white Wii Steering Wheel Controller to transform his Wii Remote Controller into a steering wheel, while the Wii Remote and Nunchuk Controller offered him a classic control. Players joined him perform speed-boosting tricks with a shake of their Wii Remote.

When they hit the road, they raced each other as their favourite Nintendo character, or even as themselves. Mario Kart Wii let them race with their personalised Mii characters, and they saw other Mii characters they created cheering from the sidelines on race courses.

Wii Sports Resorts

A whole new set of sporting activities at Wii Sports Resort! Aaron took to the beach on the tropical island of Wuhu, where he enjoyed challenges like cruising on a water scooter, duelling with swords, tossing flying discs. There were more than 18 sports games for Jeffers and his friends to try, ranging from water sports like canoeing, power cruising and wakeboarding, to ball games like basketball, bowling, table tennis and golf. Jeffers was able to take on his friend and family to find out who was strongest, fastest or most accurate.

Wii Fit Plus

AJ got Wii'lly fit with this game, using the Wii Balance Board for daily Wii Fit tests that his household could track via progress charts. He used his body to lean to block soccer balls, swivel hips to power hoop twirls or balance to hold the perfect yoga pose. His living room turned into a fitness centre for the whole family with Wii Fit and the Wii Balance Board. With Wii Fit, Jeffers' family members had fun getting a core workout, and talking about and comparing their results.

Cartoons

Wile E. Coyote (also known simply as 'The Coyote') and the Road Runner are a duo of characters from the Looney Tunes and Merrie Melodies series of cartoons. In the cartoons, the Coyote repeatedly attempts to catch and subsequently eat the Road Runner, a fast-running ground bird, but is never successful. Instead of his animal instincts, the Coyote uses absurdly complex contraptions to

pursue his prey, which comically backfired with the Coyote often getting injured in slapstick fashion. One running gag involves the Coyote trying in vain to shield himself with a little parasol against a great falling boulder that is about to crush him. Another running gag involves the coyote falling from a high cliff.

After he goes over the edge, the rest of the scene, shot from a bird's-eye view, shows the coyote falling into a canyon so deep; his figure is eventually lost to sight. This is followed a second or two later by the rising of a dust cloud from the canyon floor as the coyote hits.

Jeffers enjoyed imitating The Road Runner's sound commonly quoted as "beep, beep" in the cartoon.

Wacky Races

Who did not love that *Cannonball run*–like contest of colourful characters, vehicles and drivers of Wacky Races? But how well do you remember the 11 contestants and rides?

Dick Dastardly & Muttley In The Mean Machine, Jeffers' Saturday morning cartoon favourite. *And they're off!* It was hard for Jeffers not to root for the villains of the series, in a rocket-powered car with lots of concealed weapons. For starters, their purple dart looked a bit like a Batmobile. The Mean Machine moved like lightning with its rear rockets. Sure, they cheated all the time, but they never won. They never even crossed the finish line in the top three. Their sole aim was to win every race by hook or by crook. Drat and Double Drat! However, Jeffers could not resist Muttley's evil snickering and Dirk's moustache twirling.

Penelope Pitstop In The Compact Pussycat, a woman racer driving a pink feminine car with personal grooming facilities, zipped around in her pink beauty parlour that would sometimes backfire on the other racers - shampoo foam hitting them in their faces, for instance.

The Slag Brothers In The Boulder Mobile, Jeffers second favourite of the brightly coloured Wacky Races characters rocked along in their big chunk of granite.

The shaggy Slag Brothers inspired Captain Caveman, who came along almost a decade later.

Lazy Luke & Blubber Bear In The Arkansas Chuggabug, the Beverley Hillbellies wooden buggy driven by a coal-fired range and made bets to steer the buggy with his feet while asleep.

Professor Pat Pending In The Convert-A-Car, a mad professor with his boat like mobile. Jeffers saw Pat Pending as a clever scientist due to his Convert-a-Car having the niftiest tricks up its sleeve with a car that could change into just about anything that moved.

The Creepy Coupe, driven by The Gruesome Twosome – monsters, driving a car with a belfry; the belfry housed a dragon and various ghosts and ghouls. The Creepy Coupe was able to fly short distances through use of the dragon's wings.

The Crimson Haybailer, driven by Red Max - an air ace in a car/plane hybrid that was capable of limited flight, usually just enough to leapfrog over racers and/or obstacles in its path. The Crimson Haybailer also had a machine gun mounted, which was sporadically used.

The Army Surplus Special, driven by Sergeant Blast and Private Meekly - two soldiers racing an army jeep/tank hybrid. The Army Surplus Special made use of its tank facilities while racing, including its cannon.

The Bullet-Proof Bomb (a.k.a. The Roaring Plenty), was driven by The Ant Hill Mob (led by Clyde, with Danny, Kurby, Mac, Ring-A-Ding, Rug Bug Benny and Willy) - gangsters in a 1920s saloon car. The Turbo Terrific, driven by Peter Perfect - an All-American Jock had a crush on Penelope, so often stopped to help, driving a drag racer that regularly fell to bits.

The Buzz Wagon, driven by Rufus Ruffcut and Sawtooth - a lumberjack and a beaver in a wagon with buzzsaws for wheels, which gave it the ability to cut through almost anything, damaging or destroying the object in the process. And away they go!

Cartoon Network was one of Jeffers' all-time best TV channels for action-packed cartoons that he and his family spent endless hours laughing to and enjoying.

The best Cartoon Network TV programmes of all time for Jeffers includes the most viewed shows on Cartoon Network, 'Ed, Edd 'n' Eddy' - the series revolves around three adolescent boys: Ed, Edd 'Double Dee', and Eddy, collectively known as 'the Eds', who live in a suburban cul-de-sac in the fictional town of Peach Creek. The trio constantly invent schemes to make money from their peers to purchase their favourite confectionery and jawbreakers. Their plans usually fail, leaving them in various, often humiliating, predicaments. 'Tom & Jerry' - rivalry between the two main characters, Tom Cat and Jerry Mouse, and many recurring characters, based around slapstick comedy and 'Scooby-Doo' - this Saturday morning cartoon series featured four teenagers—Fred Jones, Daphne Blake, Velma Dinkley, and Norville 'Shaggy' Rogers—and their talking brown Great Dane dog named Scooby-Doo, who solve mysteries involving supernatural creatures through a series of antics and missteps, followed by the epic adventures of 'Johnny Bravo' - the series stars a muscular beefcake man named Johnny Bravo, who ends up in bizarre situations and adventures and is always trying to score a woman. Other classic shows include 'Dexter's Laboratory' - Dexter constantly battles against his sister Dee Dee, who always manages to gain access to his lab, despite his best efforts to keep her out. He also engages in a bitter rivalry with his neighbour and fellow-genius Mandark, and other childhood favourites like 'Dragon Ball Z, who, along with his companions, defend the Earth against villains ranging from conquerors (Vegeta, Frieza), androids (Cell) and other creatures.

Tom & Jerry

Aaron was always ready for fun and hilarious hijinx with Tom and Jerry. He would join the comedic duo in their slapstick game of cat and mouse - literally! Tom the cat is forever on the tail of Jerry the mouse - but no number of tricks, traps or frying pans will stop Jerry from a tasty lunch!

Education

Mansfield Green Junior & Infant School, Birmingham: 1995 - 2002

Joy had been collecting and gathering school commentary over the years and compiled general statements from his school (formerly Mansfield Green J & I School) reports, showcasing his performance in the classroom together with the other teachers in his year groups - from Reception to Year 6, covering English, Maths, Science and Information & Communication Technology:

Reception

"Aaron has made an excellent start to school. He is a bright, lively and enthusiastic member of the class. He is popular in class with peers and adults. Well done Aaron." – 26th June 1996.

Year 1

"Aaron is lively, outgoing and full of life. He still finds it difficult to sit for any length of time, but this has not hindered his progress this year.

He has shown that he can be very caring and considerate of others although he does tend to play a little rough sometimes. He has worked hard in all areas of the curriculum and made good progress. He particularly enjoys practical investigative activities. A good year Aaron, well done." – 25th June 1997.

Year 2

"Aaron is a popular member of the class with a wonderful sense of humour. He has worked hard this year and enjoyed learning, taking a personal pride in every aspect of his school work." – 6th July 1998.

On Jeffers' 7th birthday, his mother escorted him into Mansfield Green Community School, Birmingham, England, where he attended as a primary school pupil. When Jeffers thought his mother was kissing him goodbye, little did he know what she had in store for him.

Joy returned with a batman cake, especially made for him with candles and refreshments to celebrate and spend his special day with his class mates and teachers.

His face lit up and the smile on his face never faded – he looked so proud.

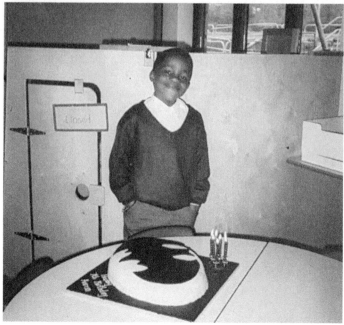

On 30th November 2001, the school's Headteacher wrote Jeffers the following letter:

"I am pleased to inform you that your application for the job of 'Postman' has been successful. You will be employed for one day per week and will work alongside another newly appointed colleague.

Your duties will include the supervision of postal sorting personnel and delivery of Christmas post to staff and pupils at Mansfield Green J&I School.

You are invited to attend a training session to be held at 12:30 p.m. on Monday 3rd December at the Year 2 Post Office. We look forward to seeing you.

Yours sincerely

Postmaster General

Year 3

"Aaron has made good progress in all aspects of his work. Aaron has a well-developed skill to solve mathematical problems and develop strategies. Aaron has also shown that he takes a great deal of pride in his work and as a result his work is always very well presented and detailed. Well done." – 13th July 1999.

On 27th April 1999, Jeffers earned himself a 'Mansfield Green J&I School Superstar Award' and gained 30 stickers for consistent good work and behaviour.

In the same year, Jeffers was presented with a 'We're Aiming Higher Award' for consistently working hard and doing his homework well, including a 'Happy Face Collector's Card with Stickers' and an 'Attendance & Timekeeping Certificate, presented to him by the school Headteacher for excellent attendance and timekeeping throughout January 1999.

ATTENDANCE & TIMEKEEPING
CERTIFICATE

Awarded to

Aaron Jeffers

For excellent Attendance and Timekeeping
throughout December 1997

Andy Knipe

Mr Andy Knipe
Headteacher

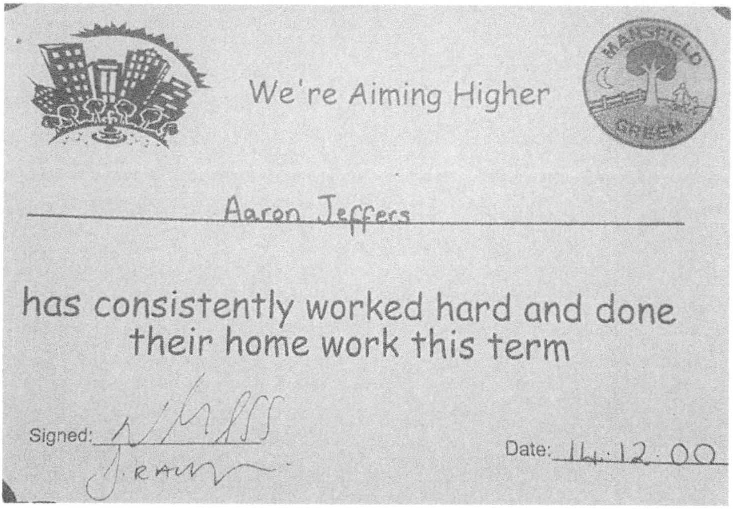

We're Aiming Higher

Aaron Jeffers

has consistently worked hard and done
their home work this term

Signed: _____

Date: 14·12·00

Year 4

"Aaron is a lively, confident member of the class. He has worked hard this year in all areas of the curriculum. Aaron is very sociable and enjoys the company of others. Aaron shows great potential. He needs to endeavour to concentrate on his work to reach his true potential." – 10th July 2000.

Year 5

"*Aaron is a lively, confident member of the class. He always takes pride in his work. Aaron can work quietly in class, but on occasions can become distracted and involved in incidents. Next year Aaron must work harder in order to achieve good levels in his SATS, which he is capable of. Aaron is a sensitive boy who responds well to praise. I wish him well for next year.*" – *29th June 2001.*

Year 6

"Aaron takes pride in the presentation of his work but needs to work more quickly in all subjects. Activities are often unfinished because he seems unable to concentrate for a sustained length of time. He must not let himself be distracted by others, yet he must also allow others to do their work too. He is pleasant and well-mannered." – 5th July 2002.

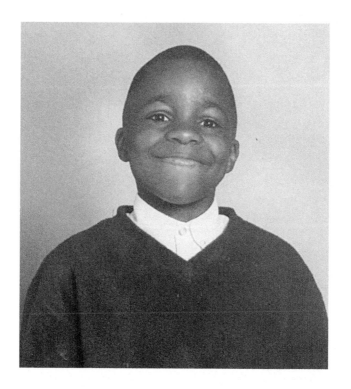

It was after Jeffers' committal the school wrote a tribute to the inspiring young man on his Facebook page:

*"A lovely send-off to a much loved young man **Aaron Jeffers**, as evidenced today you will be clearly missed, but even more obvious you will never be forgotten, wherever you went you left a lasting impression and as mentioned today it just had to be written for all to read." 4th April 2014 @ 19:56.*

Mansfield Green Junior & Infant School Awards & Certificates

sack

1st

This is to certify that

Aaron

won the race

Signed: _____

Date: 16.7.97

running

2nd

This is to certify that

Aaron

came second

Signed: _____

Date: 16.7.97

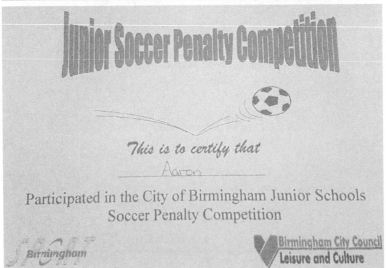

Junior Soccer Penalty Competition

This is to certify that

Aaron

Participated in the City of Birmingham Junior Schools
Soccer Penalty Competition

Birmingham

Birmingham City Council
Leisure and Culture

Thank You

Aaron Jeffers

for taking part in the

"Design an Egg"
Competition

Well Done

Signed : *Mr Andy Knipe*   Date :   3rd April 1998

ASTON MANOR SCHOOL
CERTIFICATE OF MERIT
SPRING TERM 2001

Awarded to _____ of Mansfield Green School

for successfully taking part in a

LITERACY INSPIRE WORKSHOP

on Thursday March 29th 2001

Headteacher

After-School Club

As a full-time working parent, Aston Play Centre was Joy's lifeline. She was so happy with the facilities there that she sent her young boy to after-school club, extending the school day from 8am until 6pm. Aaron attended Aston Park Play Centre, Trinity Road, Aston, Birmingham between the ages of 5 to 11 years, 5 days a week from 15:30 p.m. until 6:00 p.m. during school term.

A lovely park play centre situated within the main Aston Park. With a roundabout, at least 2 slides, monkey bars, a see-saw and an outdoor play gym, it was the place for Aaron to be on a dry sunny day after school. An especially pretty place to be in the summer and a short walk to the gorgeous Aston Hall and its beautiful gardens. Aston Park Play Centre opened in 1997 and operated from a purpose-built play centre in Aston Park in Birmingham.

AJ attended Aston Play Centre for a variety of sessions. He had a very good awareness of healthy eating as well as the importance of good nutrition from a young age through planned activities such as food tasting, and participated in a Ready, Steady, Cook session in 2001.

As a child and team member, Aaron was offered a light snack of toast with a drink and helped himself to water throughout the sessions. He enjoyed the social interaction that took place during snack time with his peers and staff, as he talked to staff about his day at school and about activities they had planned to do.

Aaron enjoyed a wide range of activities, both indoors and outdoors which helped to promote his physical development. His favourite time of the day was participating in outdoor activities such as football, dodge ball, basketball, movement and dance, and talked excitedly about enjoying these activities. Aaron also looked forward to using his manipulative skills by using scissors, spatulas and paint brushes. Entering the setting was exciting for Aaron as he was eager to participate in the activities on offer as staff prepared the rooms before he arrived.

AJ really enjoyed his time in Aston Play Centre. He achieved well in his development and leisure as a result of the staff's clear understanding of how children learn and the importance of play. Activities such as cooking, ironing and sewing enabled Aaron to learn skills to prepare him for life when he grew older, whilst developing his self-esteem and confidence. He spent his time purposefully as he concentrated and became engrossed in creative activities such as drawing and colouring. Aaron accessed books for pleasure or to research topics as part of his projects. He enjoyed sitting and chatting with friends and staff. Staff was very friendly, and the atmosphere was good too.

Knowing Aston Play Centre was Ofsted-regulated, meant it was the only way that Jeffers' mother could find safe, affordable childcare for her son.

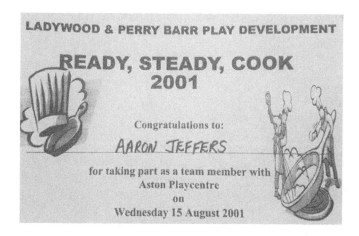

George Dixon International School, Edgbaston, Birmingham: 2003 – 2008

National Curriculum

Jeffers was well known for being clean, smart and well presented. He was seen to be self-motivated and someone who could perform well at a high level, completing homework set and praise earned for his achievements.

Teachers were very pleased with the presentation and standard of his work and commented on how he achieved a consistently high standard.

He showed considerable interest in Information Technology and used computer hardware with confidence as well as used a variety of software unaided in order to complete tasks. Jeffers also showed interest in Art and Design Technology.

Speaking and listening was what Jeffers enjoyed doing during his English lessons, conveying meaning to the teacher or a group of pupils whilst relating real or imaginary events in a connected narrative. He participated as speaker and listener in group discussions

or activities, expressing a personal view and commenting constructively on what was being discussed or experienced. During group work, he would make a valuable contribution to the activities, make useful suggestions and was fully involved in practical work.

In drama, Jeffers worked easily with others, and was naturally respectful and willing to take on board other students' suggestions for shaping the drama.

He sometimes accepted the responsibility of leadership in the organisation of the group. The creative student coped well if disagreements occurred within the group.

School Friendships

As with any relationship, friendships bring support and joy and occasionally strife. A very special friendship began to develop between Jeffers and a group of 4 other students.

During the first few months at school, Jeffers and one of the students from the group, named Luntu, did not get on very well, as he had just arrived in England from Africa – still fresh in the UK. Jeffers had a thing about 'mimicking' other people and 'dissing' them – all part and parcel of childhood and growing up. Jeffers was a 'great mimicker.' The group of students (Luntu, Dhillon, Nicholas and

Peter) were all sort of scared of being imitated by the impersonator because when some of his peers received a taste of his 'dissing' all they wanted to do was 'crawl into a hole.' Two of the much closer students, including Jeffers, were in the same form class, so they would see each other every morning and afternoon, whereas the remaining 2 would not.

On one occasion, Jeffers almost fought Luntu, the newly arrived student from Africa. Luntu's mother had bought him a new pair of football boots, which Jeffers decided he was going to wear in the school canteen. When the young student realised, he discovered Jeffers had worn his football boots to kick a ball. The furious student was very sensitive to Jeffers' actions and asked him, *"Why are you wearing my football boots?"*

Jeffers began to imitate Luntu's African accent and replied, *"Why you wearing my boots man!?!?!?"* Jeffers just knew how to get under somebody else's skin, literally and irritated the student. He continued to run around in circles playing football with the student's football boots on, chasing the angry and vexed student, who wanted so badly to beat Jeffers up. At the same time, raged Luntu squashed how he then felt towards Jeffers, as he realised this was how youngsters pranked around.

The dynamics of the group changed with greater maturity during secondary school. What really got the young boys' relationship connected was football – that is what really united Jeffers and the group of boys. They really loved the sport. Jeffers was very fast and a good finisher. Jeffers and 2 of the young men were much closer to one another, and the 2 other youngsters were much closer to each other.

As the young men began to grow up, their friendship and bond started to become a lot more mature – it was not just 'dissing' taking place.

Jeffers, Peter and Nicholas began arranging sleepovers between them at each other's homes. They would play FIFA sessions for endless hours on the weekends to no end.

The young men's circle of friendship split up during Year 9 and 10 at secondary school. Jeffers developed his own circle of friends, and so did the other teenagers, however their strong bond was still present with regular 'catch-ups.'

After college, Luntu, now a Film Producer, reunited with Jeffers in ASDA Perry Barr, Birmingham in 2013. He described Jeffers as a '*grown man*' and '*mature.*' Luntu explained:

"*Everyone loved Jeffers. I could see the way he was serving the customers, and everyone was greeting him. I was so amazed to see him turn out to be the young man he was.*"

Shortly after the brief sighting of Jeffers in ASDA Perry Barr, Luntu, Peter and Nicholas arranged a reunion at Jeffers' home and had a fun 'catch up' session. It was the first time the young men had all seen each other in years properly –3 of them just together. Each of the young men felt it was incredible just to see how much they had matured and grown. Luntu explained Jeffers was still very energetic, but as always, they felt Jeffers was very skilled at mimicking others.

Luntu added, "*He could mimic anything and anyone and Jeffers would get it spot on – he had a natural ability to mimic others. Jeffers' strength was with people as he was such a great observer of people and he understood the mannerisms of others. Jeffers was so good at storytelling and over-reacting, telling stories repeatedly and selling his story to others.*"

2013 was the last time the young men saw each other and planned to see each other again. The men later heard Jeffers had passed on. Luntu reported in a video interview with Joy:

"*It has been hard for me, Peter, Dhillon and Nicholas to contribute towards this book because we have not healed from Jeffers' passing – it is still very raw - a shock although it happened 6 years ago – it still hits home. For some of us, losing Jeffers was our first time losing someone; a friend we grew up with or someone we were so close to – Jeffers was so young and ambitious. We did not know how to react to it even up to the present day. It is hard for me and the rest of the guys to deal with the sad loss of Jeffers.*

Some of Jeffers' friends miss him so much that they have tattoos on their chest to prove what Jeffers' friendship meant to them. Jeffers brought so much life around his group of school friends. He was so lively, bubbly – always happy. He was the 'joker' and was extremely funny."

For the last 6 years, and on each anniversary of Aaron's death, the young men - Luntu, Dhillon, Peter and Nicholas - take the time to visit AJ at his resting place to pay their respects and to remember their school mate.

Physical Education & Clubs

A high-quality physical education curriculum inspires all pupils to succeed and excel in competitive sport and other physically-demanding activities. It provided Aaron with opportunities to become physically confident in a way which supported his health and fitness. In addition, it provided him with opportunities to compete in sport and other activities to help build his character and help to embed values such as fairness and respect.

Playing football was a popular and successful sport at George Dixon Academy (formerly George Dixon International School & Sixth Form).

The school ensured that every pupil had the opportunity to play in competitive matches and tournaments, and that full-time footballers enjoyed a busy schedule, playing teams from all the local community. The football lover competed in an array of competitions and tournaments on behalf of the School Football Team, interspersed with numerous friendly games.

Jeffers expressed his wish to excel in football and was nurtured by a full-time Coach. He showed promise and was put into the Sports Leadership Programme, which included both guided and peer-to-peer learning and supervised leadership to ensure that he had all the required skills he needed to lead basic physical activities to other people.

In 2007, the young footballer decided to undertake a qualification in Sports Leadership, where he learned and demonstrated important life skills such as effective communication, leadership skills including organisation, planning and teamwork through the medium of sport, whilst learning to lead basic physical activities to others as part of the

School Football Team. Over time, he became a confident, healthy leader through sport and physical activity.

The course enabled Jeffers to deliver structured and inclusive sport and physical activity sessions to students. The sessions used sport to deliver fun and engaging physical activities with other students, where he planned, lead and evaluated sports/physical activity sessions over a few tutored hours and then demonstrated his leadership skills as part of his assessment.

On 27th July 2007, Jeffers gained a Level 1 Award in Sports Leadership (with Grade Merit), enabling successful learners to assist in leading purposeful and enjoyable sport or physical activity, under direct supervision.

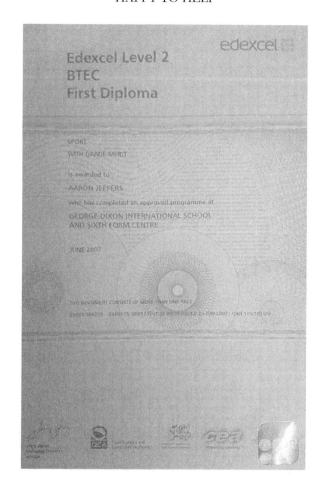

Night Life

Birmingham is home to some of the sexiest, most stylish R&B clubs in the UK; with an army of resident DJs and guest hosts, the city seems dedicated to bringing party goers the best R&B jams around.

Celebrating and partying with friends is what Jeffers enjoyed. Watching international DJs and dancing all night was his fix. It was a very powerful cause of enjoyment and why he went to nightclubs with his friends due to dance culture. He had an inherent enjoyment of dance and incorporated dance as a large aspect of entertainment and socialisation.

A further potential reason behind why Aaron went to nightclubs was to express himself and have fun. When he went on nights out, he dressed up and made sure that he looked his best.

Birmingham Metropolitan College –

James Watt Campus

Between the years of 2007 – 2009 brought a series of new skills for Jeffers.

Expanding his personal development, Jeffers branched out into fitness and began attending gym activities to enhance his health and fitness levels, plus keep up his stamina during sports and much more.

Jeffers had a gym membership where he worked out in stunning exercise studios, to state-of-the-art gyms and facilities, packed full of top-quality fitness equipment so there was always something new for him to try.

The most common reasons why Jeffers started going to the gym and lifting weights was to get 'ripped' or 'swole'; challenge himself – knowing that he had made progress and feeling good about himself – happy feeling to release those well-known happy chemicals: endorphins. He had commitment, discipline and guts; all of which got stronger along with his muscles as he consistently got his reps in.

Matthew Boulton College, Birmingham

During his next fitness journey, Jeffers became hands-on behind the scenes. He gained a varying degree of knowledge around general fitness involved in exercise prescription and instruction, including learning how to motivate clients by setting goals and providing feedback and accountability to clients as well as measure client's strengths and weaknesses with fitness assessments. For his efforts, sports fan Aaron achieved a Level 3 Personal Trainer qualification at Matthew Boulton College on 11th September 2009.

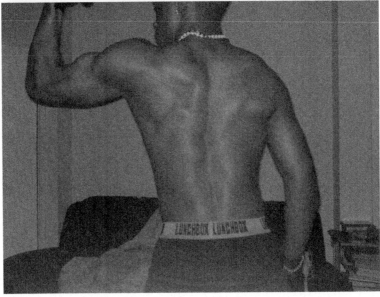

Sporting Achievements

Joy is extremely proud of her talented son for his sportsmanship and numerous sporting achievements and would always share how delighted she was with him. Jeffers possessed an impressive list of awards at varying levels. Below are images showcasing Jeffers' major achievements in the sports industry:

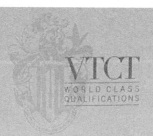

VTCT
WORLD CLASS
QUALIFICATIONS

This is to certify that

Aaron Jeffers

has satisfied the requirements for the qualification of

Level 3 Certificate in
Swedish Massage
(100/6160/5)

Date: 27 Jul 2008

Registration No: 704707

The award of this qualification is based on the successful attainment of the National
Standards in units of competence as detailed on a Record of Achievement and/or one of
more Certificates of Unit Credit.

Susan Brakewell
Susan Brakewell
Acting Chief Executive
VTCT

The regulatory logo on this certificate indicates the qualification is accredited for England,
Wales and Northern Ireland.

Ofqual

00104824

VTCT
WORLD CLASS
QUALIFICATIONS

This is to certify that

Aaron Jeffers

has completed the following units from within the named qualification:

Level 3 Certificate in
Swedish Massage
(100/6160/5)

Units completed:

VR17   Prepare for and provide body massage

Date: 27 Jul 2008   Registration No: 704707

Susan Brakewell
Susan Brakewell
Acting Chief Executive
VTCT

The regulatory logo on this certificate indicates the qualification is accredited for England,
Wales and Northern Ireland.

Ofqual

00639729

This is to certify that

Aaron Jeffers

has completed the following units from within the named qualification:

Level 3 Diploma in
Health, Safety, Security
and Employment Standards (500/1048/7)

Units completed:

VR02 Support health, safety and security in the workplace
VR74 Support employment standards

Date: 27 Jul 2008   Registration No: 704707

Susan Brakewell
Susan Brakewell
Acting Chief Executive
VTCT

The regulatory logo on this certificate indicates the qualification is accredited for England,
Wales and Northern Ireland.

00039730

71

This is to certify that

Aaron Jeffers

has satisfied the requirements for the qualification of

Level 3 Diploma in
Health, Safety, Security
and Employment Standards (500/1048/7)

Date: 27 Jul 2008   Registration No: 704707

The award of this qualification is based on the successful attainment of the National
Standards in units of competence as detailed on a Record of Achievement and/or one of
more Certificates of Unit Credit.

Susan Brakewell
Susan Brakewell
Acting Chief Executive
VTCT

The regulatory logo on this certificate indicates the qualification is accredited for England,
Wales and Northern Ireland.

00104825

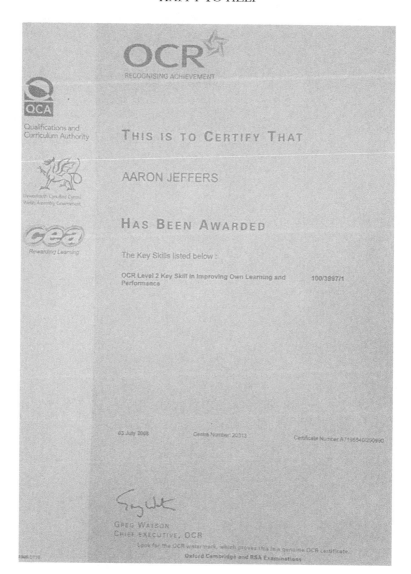

OCR
RECOGNISING ACHIEVEMENT

Qualifications and
Curriculum Authority

Llywodraeth Cynulliad Cymru
Welsh Assembly Government

cea
Rewarding Learning

THIS IS TO CERTIFY THAT

AARON JEFFERS

HAS BEEN AWARDED

the following unit/s from the
OCR Level 2 Certificate in Teaching Exercise and Fitness

Promote healthy living — M/100/6841
Demonstrate knowledge of the exercise and fitness work environment — T/100/6842
Plan and teach a gym session — F/100/6844

This certificate has been issued to mark the attainment of units within an accredited qualification and does not mark the attainment of the full qualification itself.

04 August 2008   Centre Number: 20051   Certificate Number A7528562/290890
Accreditation number for full qualification: 100/1075/9

GREG WATSON
CHIEF EXECUTIVE, OCR
Look for the OCR watermark, which proves this is a genuine OCR certificate.
Oxford Cambridge and RSA Examinations

A982 0624

74

This is to certify that

AARON JEFFERS

Has been awarded the following

NCFE LEVEL 2 CERTIFICATE IN FITNESS INDUSTRY STUDIES

This achievement included the successful completion of the units detailed
on the Candidate Unit Summary

Date Awarded:	11/08/2008
Centre No:	020051
Accreditation No:	100/1197/3
Session:	2007/2008
Candidate No:	50785905
Certificate No:	F058977

David Grailey
Chief Executive
NCFE

Chris Hughes CBE
Chair
NCFE

OCA Qualifications and
Curriculum Authority

CANDIDATE UNIT SUMMARY

AARON JEFFERS

Has achieved the following components of

NCFE LEVEL 2 CERTIFICATE IN FITNESS INDUSTRY STUDIES

Internal Assessment Fully Achieved

Units Achieved

D/100/8486   CREATE AND MAINTAIN CUSTOMER EXCELLENCE

H/100/8487   SHOW A BASIC UNDERSTANDING OF ANATOMY, PHYSIOLOGY AND NUTRITION

K/100/8488   PROMOTE SAFE WORKING PRACTICE

M/100/8489   UNDERSTAND COMPONENTS OF PHYSICAL FITNESS AND PRINCIPLES OF TRAINING

H/100/8490   DEVISE AND DELIVER A TRAINING SESSION

T/100/8493   PROVIDE A RECEPTION SERVICE

External Assessment Not Applicable

Date Awarded: 11 August 2008

Centre No: 020051

Accreditation No: 100/1197/3

Session: 2007/2008

Candidate No: 60765905

David Gralley
Chief Executive
NCFE

Chris Hughes
Chair
NCFE

QCA   Qualifications and Curriculum Authority

cea   Rewarding Learning

ncfe

This is to certify that

AARON JEFFERS

Has been awarded the following

NCFE LEVEL 2 CERTIFICATE IN NUTRITION AND HEALTH

This achievement included the successful completion of the units detailed on the Candidate Unit Summary

Date Awarded: 15/09/2008
Centre No: 020051
Accreditation No: 100/4425/7
Session: 2007/2008
Candidate No: 59825757
Certificate No: F990360

David Grailey
Chief Executive
NCFE

Chris Hughes CBE
Chair
NCFE

Ofqual

Llywodraeth Cynulliad Cymru
Welsh Assembly Government

Rewarding Learning

ncfe

CANDIDATE UNIT SUMMARY

AARON JEFFERS

Has achieved the following components of

NCFE LEVEL 2 CERTIFICATE IN NUTRITION AND HEALTH

Internal Assessment Fully Achieved

Units Achieved

A/102/6736	EXPLORE PRINCIPLES OF HEALTHY EATING
F/102/6737	CONSIDER NUTRITIONAL NEEDS OF A VARIETY OF INDIVIDUALS
J/102/6738	USE FOOD AND NUTRITION INFORMATION TO PLAN A HEALTHY DIET

External Assessment Not Applicable

Date Awarded:	10 September 2009
Centre No:	020051
Accreditation No:	100/4426/7
Session:	2007/2009
Candidate No:	50825757

David Grailey
Chief Executive
NCFE

Chris Hughes
Chair
NCFE

Ofqual

www.ncfe.org.uk

Blossoming College Friendships

If someone asked Jeffers today how many friends from college he saw on a regular basis, he would say that his friends were still all in touch with one another. The friends AJ made in college also ended up being his lifelong friends.

In college, there was an instant affinity formed among Aaron and his friends, owing to the fact that they had all just been kids taking the next big step in to adulthood. Jeffers believed his college friendships were the best friendships he had because they laid the foundation of all his future friendships, and yes, even his personal relationships.

Jeffers and his college friends, Paul and Joel bonded for life, because they had practically seen each other day in, day out. They saw each other's faces, but still found a way to co-exist and live peacefully together. They spent a lot of time together - played PlayStation; laughed together; drove together; partied and drank together. Now that is a lot of bonding time!!

The boys also witnessed one another's messes, both the personal and physical kind, and had been there for each other. The lads patiently sat through all those years of studying hard at college to achieve their goals and aspirations. If that is not the best kind of friendship, I do not know what is.

The boys had done a lot of growing up together. They stuck together during the really tough days studying for exams and meeting deadlines. The students had figured out together what they wanted to do with our lives after college. Now, looking back, they realised that they were still friends who continued to purse their life plans. That is how you know this trio are friends for life.

After Aaron's demise, his Course Tutor, Tracey Need, from Birmingham Metropolitan College reflected on a very fond memory of him and wrote:

"One of Aaron's best traits was that he loved to laugh and smile. Whenever one of his college mates was feeling down and needed a friend to lean on, he was there to support them.

My fondest memory of Aaron is a very personal one. My mother was terminally ill at the time. Aaron stayed behind after a lesson and asked if I was okay, then asked could he help, as he had detected I seemed distracted. Without going into too much detail, I explained the situation and Aaron sat and listened in a very mature and respectful manner, asking if there was anything he could do to help?

The following day Aaron arrived in my lesson with flowers and a little card with a poem on it relating to the love a child has for its mother. That conversation and Aaron's kindness has stayed with me and will never be forgotten.

Aaron was a very kind and considerate young man. To this day I can still picture his amazing smile. God bless you young man."

One of Jeffers' unemployed college friends, Joel crafted a cover letter; tweaked his resume, and finally applied to a retail position at the ASDA Perry Barr store. Jeffers helped Joel land a job in ASDA Perry Barr, and was able to recommend him because he had first-hand knowledge of his workmate's skills and abilities, plus Jeffers shared his awareness of both the company and what the job entailed that his associate applied for. With the guidance Aaron provided Joel, he now knew what he needed to do. It was time to get ready for that interview and make a good first and lasting impression on the ASDA Hiring Manager! Getting the job offer was cause for a celebration. Joel, the Store Assistant, did extremely well in that position. Joy is absolutely certain that Aaron must have given Joel a hearty pat on his back for his well-deserved efforts.

Career

2009 – 2013 Retail Success

Jeffers was discovered by ASDA Perry Barr, Birmingham who interviewed him while recruiting for new talent. Aaron began working at ASDA in Perry Barr, Birmingham at the tender age of 19, as a Store Colleague - Self Checkout Host on a part-time basis. He participated in lots of over-time and his attendance was excellent up until he turned ill.

Shortly after starting his new job, he made ASDA headlines in 2009 for the genuinely warm and friendly way he served customers at the checkout. At the supermarket, Aaron held several jobs which varied from deterring theft by way of receipt checks as well as greeting and thanking the customer; marking returns with printed labels; excellent courtesy and store knowledge was always a must to remaining courteous especially whilst distinguishing whether customers had paid/unpaid for items.

He played a major part in making customers' shopping experience a fantastic one. With his stunning outgoing personality, politeness, communication, patience, helpfulness, smart appearance and calm nature he had the vital ingredients that made a difference to customers leaving ASDA with a smile and feeling that they could not wait to return again soon.

The youngster was outgoing and simply got along with and supported others. If truth be told, Jeffers enjoyed working on the automated self-service checkouts which enabled customers to scan, bag and pay for items themselves, as well as be in complete control throughout their shopping experience.

Every day the ambitious young man had a smile in his voice as well as on his face with his super white teeth.

Courtesy is a big part of ASDA's warm and friendly service culture, and Aaron always said *"hello"* and *"goodbye"* – and in between listened and showed an interest to ascertain customers' needs.

Customers were greeted with a smile and he always paid full attention to the customers he served, taking them to where a product was located when they asked and ensuring he had an adequate supply of 'Bags for Life' carrier bags for customers.

The Store Colleague - Self Checkout Host skilfully managed all 14 self-service checkouts during peak times, conducting daily checks to ensure the touch screen monitors, the exterior and the scanner scale were all clean. He even devised a set of instructions for his colleagues to follow so that they knew what to do and who to contact in the event of a problem occurring. Jeffers wanted his colleagues to be the very best they could be and knowledgeable on the self-service checkouts, having peace of mind that if he was not in store, that his team could function smoothly without him. Jeffers did extraordinarily well in everything that he put his mind to, and was an asset to ASDA Perry Barr, Birmingham.

ASDA Perry Barr Pay Tribute To Jeffers

Photos are a beautiful and treasured reminder of loved ones who are gone. Photos preserve memories like pre-school graduations, birthday parties, kids posing happily with artistic creations, weddings, etc. We know these moments are fleeting and in time our brain will no longer be able to remember them with the same vivid imagery, so we take photos.

Photos can make us smile, laugh, cry and remember. One of the most difficult things about losing someone is the feeling that their memory is fading. Their smell, voice, and the feeling of their embrace – we wish for them to appear in a dream just so we can remember these things again. Photos are an accurate and literal reminder of our loved ones.

In honour and remembrance of Aaron, ASDA Perry Barr has prominently displayed the photo below of Jeffers as a tribute for the last 6 years on the self-scan and go checkouts, which he used to manage. This is to honour and give Jeffers his place of prominence in the ASDA Store. Jeffers' work colleagues and ASDA customers still consider Aaron to be a part of them. He exists in their memory and he continues to influence people to this day.

Whether Aaron's photo sits on the self-scan tills has no bearing on his prominence in the ASDA Store; but memories and moments involving Aaron are an important part of their lives.

Jeffers will also give future generations a chance to connect with their deceased ancestors and family history. How else will Jeffers' son know whether he has his father's handsome and gorgeous looks?

The photo above showcases Aaron representing his employer at ASDA Sunday League Football matches regularly scoring superb goals. He was truly the man of the show.

The young man was a conscientious team member of the ASDA workforce, attracting so many customers into the store with his stunning personality and exceptional customer service – also earning himself numerous 'Happy To Help Awards/ABC Star Points' for his efforts.

Jeffers became a First Aider on the 5th March 2013 and completed 'ASDA's Caring For Our Customers' Briefing on the 19th September 2012. He made his mother extremely proud.

Swaggy Dresser, Snapback Hats

Jeffers was a perfectionist and was known for taking pride in his appearance. The new generation originally use 'swag' to describe anyone thought to carry themselves in a way considered by some to be sexy or cool.

For those of you who knew Jeffers, you will know that he was a snapback hat lover. Aaron had a variety of snapback hats included in his collection. With their distinctive flat brim look, snapbacks were a great statement accessory for Jeffers – which he perfectly perched on top of his head.

Thanks to the biggest hip-hop artists like Tupac Shakur, Ice Cube and Dr. Dre who advertised the snapback, it did not take Jeffers long to fall in love with the style, when the snapback became one of the biggest trends in the '90s.

Check out a few of Jeffers' snapback hat collection from Hatman here:

Jeffers would also stay stylishly snug and also topped off his street look with his collection of Nike and Adidas beanie hats, purchased from JD Sports, to keep him warm during those winter months.

He would check in with his mother for his fortnightly haircuts, ensuring he had his hairbrush to hand to keep his hair, side burns and goatee well groomed.

Jeffers always carried a small tub of Vaseline in his trouser pocket to protect his hands, particularly during his daily shifts at the ASDA store.

Trainers

Jeffers was always on the hunt for killer trainers. When it came to choosing the right pair, looking at his current wardrobe, especially his favourite pieces, was always a good place to start.

Jeffers thought about styles and colourways what would compliment what he already loved to wear, to dress down smarter looks or elevate a simple outfit.

With the criteria in mind: style, comfort, quality and originality, Jeffers applied these simple rules to help him find the perfect pair of trainers to suit his personal taste.

For Jeffers, Converse delivered on essential sneaks! Converse kept him looking fresh with a full array of statement styles and classic designs, no matter where he wore them.

From iconic high tops to signature low top styles, Jeffers copped the latest Converse trainers to ensure his footwear was always on point. There was nothing wrong with a classic pair of grey Converse, however when Jeffers was itching to add a little pizzazz, he just doubled up on different coloured laces depending on what he was wearing and continued crossing over, lacing through every other pair of eyelets on his Converse.

Jeffers used coloured laces to completely transform the look of his shoes, as well as his 'on fleek' outfits from boring to stunning!

Jeffers also switched up his footwear sporting these black and white colourways with a thick contrast rubber sole and 3 white stripes branding to the sidewall of the Nizza collection from Adidas Originals. Originally droppin' as a court sneaker, these creps have gone from shootin' hoops to stylin' up the streets. Bringin' a clean, minimal and lightweight look with a canvas upper, these back-to-basics sneakers were Jeffers everyday essentials. Another brand of trainer Jeffers stocked up on was the Nike's Blazers, with its signature basketball-inspired design on each style, which made them classic, while vibrant prints and supple finishes showed off a modern style. They matched any outfit and allowed Jeffers to stand out in a crowd.

Jury Service

ASDA Perry Barr granted Jeffers the right to take time off work to serve on a jury. The young juror was sworn in on criminal trials for Jury Service at Birmingham Magistrates Court during 3rd – 14th October 2011. He acted as the foreperson of the jury and his role was to write the jury's decision (guilty or not guilty) against the charges on the Issue Paper (a form that the charges against the defendants are listed on) and announce the verdict in open court. Aaron and a few strangers were given collective power over another person's future.

They all had to decide whether they were lying, whether the witnesses were credible and how to interpret the evidence.

Because those strangers were the only people with whom Aaron could discuss the case, he became quickly bonded to them. They only just met but they all shared the same secret. The idea was that the group represented a cross-section of the society potentially wronged by the actions of the defendant.

Jeffers shared with his mother how he thoroughly enjoyed every second of it. In his experience, serving on a jury was extremely interesting and a fascinating experience, well worth the investment of time and attention. Aaron found it incredibly engaging, and even challenging.

ASDA Colleagues' Statements

"Well what can I say about Aaron? So many things. He was a star and still is. He was always so happy and always had a smile on his face. He always used to say, "How's it going?" and give me a huge hug. If there was anything you needed help with, Aaron would always be willing to help, and he certainly did. I miss Aaron so much and there is not one day that goes by where I don't think about him. He loved his football. He had so much going for him. Aaron was an inspiration and loved by so many."

"The first thing you noticed about Aaron was his smile. He had the biggest smile ever. He welcomed everyone, colleagues and customers alike. He was very popular with anyone who met him. Injustice of any kind against anyone he knew really upset him, and he would rush to support them. I remember the day when he came into work and announced to everyone, even the customers that he was going to become a father. Proud does not cover it. He just could not wait to become a daddy. We still miss him greatly and the light left ASDA when he did. A shining light sent to bring joy to people."

"Aaron was the best dressed here at ASDA Perry Barr. He was always clean and immaculate. He always said, "hello and goodbye"; he was pleasant and always took part in ASDA events."

"Aaron was in the ASDA Football Team and used to attend every Sunday for football practice. Aaron played forward and striker position for the team and ASDA staff used to play with him. He was very strong on the pitch, was a team player and very skilful in football. He had an incredible speed on the pitch. At football matches Aaron was very competitive, scoring loads of goals which made both Aaron and ASDA staff very happy. I knew his family very well in Aston, Birmingham and from that moment we became united and stuck together no matter what. He was a friendly, bubbly and very chatty individual. He smiled a lot and had a good attitude. The best times ever were when we had social and physical interaction. It is not the same anymore – I miss those days. He used to play table tennis with me at break times in the ASDA Staff Room – he was very good at it. We used to crack jokes too. Negative customers coming into the store would get at Aaron for no reason. He would come up to the Staff Room and talk to me about his experiences to calm himself down. I miss his hugs and touches (firms). He was like my brother. We even talked about religion and peace.

Aaron used to say mothers are everything. He asked me questions about culture, fasting, Ramadan and even fasted himself to see what others went through. His funeral was attended by over 1,000 people. Aaron was regarded as a well-respected person and a hero. I had a dream about Aaron after he passed on. As he waved at me from a bus, he wore white golf gloves."

"I am the ASDA Cook. Aaron used to love my steak pie and would put tomato sauce on everything. He told everyone in store "that pie was boom". He would crack jokes when eating his food with his big massive grin across his face and loved his Caribbean food."

"We used to think Aaron had shares in 'Subway'. That boy used to eat Subways like no one's business. We used to say to him "Subway again Aaron". Absolutely fantastic guy."

"When ASDA customers saw the announcement of Aaron's death displayed on a table at the entrance to the store, they thought he had won another award and did not realise what had taken place. Customers became alarmed and started to break down, screaming in store. ASDA colleagues were alerted to the screams and began consoling and comforting the customers, offering them consoling words. Everyone was devastated. ASDA colleagues who had left the store and obtained jobs elsewhere turned up to Aaron's funeral, from Wales, London and different parts of the country, as did the regular customers who did their weekly shopping in store. ASDA Perry Barr had to loan colleagues from other stores to provide staff cover on the day of Aaron's funeral on 4th April 2014. His funeral was attended by over 1,000 people. Aaron was a hero and well respected."

"Aaron was the life and soul of the party. He was helpful and polite to both staff and the customers."

"Miss Aaron Jeffers every day. Loved him to bits. He was like my brother. Loved his jokes and will never forget that I could never keep up with him in football."

Personal Life

Family

To Aaron, family meant everything, feeling secure and loved, to have someone who he could count on, who he could share his problems with, listen to and support him. But it also meant showing respect for each other and a sense of belonging.

What family meant to Jeffers was love and someone that would always be there for him through the good times and the bad. It was about encouragement, understanding, hope, comfort, advice, values and morals. These things were all important to Aaron because it made him feel secure and happy inside regardless of what was going on in his life.

Following family traditions showcases the importance of family, as well. Family traditions are experiences that Jeffers created together with his family on a regular basis, whether these involved family gatherings, eating out, celebrations or even attending events together. Not only did these experiences create memories for years to come, they also gave Jeffers and his family members a stronger sense of belonging.

What made Jeffers' family gatherings so special was letting him spend quality time with his relatives which helped develop his social skills and also helped him build a rapport for himself among most of the members of his family tree.

Jeffers looked up to his relatives. He loved the stories narrated to him by older relatives. The stories he heard gave him insight into what he would face later on in life when he was supposed to overcome challenges that came his way. The older generation in Aaron's family served as his role models throughout his life, who he turned to when he faced a problem.

Whenever Jeffers' family found conducive moments to come together, many positive things or changes happened. Family gatherings helped to reunite broken relationships between Jeffers' family members.

The best moment to solve all grievances is when the family came together. It helped to settle down any dispute among family members.

There was nothing Jeffers looked forward to more than spending quality time with his family because he adored them. His absolute greatest joy was the love of food at family gatherings. Boy did he love Caribbean food: fried chicken, white rice and veg, Jamaican chicken and pumpkin soup with dumplings, salmon, mutton rice and peas, fried hake fish served with white rice and festival/fried dumplings. He would lick every finger in sheer delight.

It was at family gatherings and in the long after dinner conversations that Jeffers learned about his family history. Jeffers was very fond of his family and always spoke very highly of his grandparents. He enjoyed spending time with them for the simple reason they made him laugh and always had amusing stories and jokes to share and tell.

Aaron told everyone he could not wait to become a father and was so excited about the imminent birth of his first child.

He spoke very highly about his son to everyone that had the pleasure of knowing how much becoming a father meant to him.

Mischievous Personality

Playful people enjoy teasing, wordplay, improvising and taking challenges in a light-hearted way. They enjoy unusual things and are good at creating environments for others to enjoy.

Everyone loves knowing someone with a playful, mischievous mind-set and attitude. Some people are naturally more spontaneous and playful than others, but anyone can learn how to spice up a situation with some mischief. Risk taking is a critical aspect of being mischievous. Live to your fullest potential by not worrying too much about the consequences. Every seemingly normal situation can be made funnier and more interesting when you add some mischief, and that is what Aaron did. He liked having fun by playing harmless tricks on people.

Here Jeffers is pictured below dressed up in his younger cousin's (Shakeel's) hooded body warmer, wearing a random pair of nerdy glasses that made him look super cool.

Death, Sickness & Family Breakdown

The death of Jeffers' grandad on his father's side of the family came to him as a huge shock on 29th June 2007 at a time in his life when he was still young, just 17. He often wanted to be more with his friends than family for support. He found the intensity of emotion overwhelming and was not able to find the words or ways to talk about his feelings and emotions with others. Jeffers felt he was coping, and wanted to be seen to be, but inside he was hurting a great deal and brushing his emotions under the carpet hoping they would go away.

For comfort Jeffers would often visit and spend time with his loved one – Grandfather at Witton Cemetery, Birmingham. In a statement, Aaron wrote on his Facebook page:

"Grandad that day u died has come and gone twice nw an I still ent over it

. If I cud tlk to u and tell u I love u 1 last time I wud
.

I'd do nufin to have that chance. I miss you bare man, seein u bein put in tha ground mde me realise I'm never guna see u agen. If we cud trade placez I'd be

whre u are
. RIP Grandad. Cnt wait to see u agen. I fink abt u each day. Happy 84th Birthday. Love u and cnt wait to see u agen. RIP.

When Jeffers' grandfather, Cephas on his mother's side became critically ill with a number of strokes and seizures, it affected him and his entire family. Joy observed how Jeffers reacted differently to the news of his grandfather's illness and said he had found it difficult to see Cephas so ill and weak.

Everyone in Jeffers family was affected and they were all dealing with the unknown, using strengths and emotions they did not even know they had. Most of us are not taught how to manage when someone we love is very ill, let alone how to support children, teens and young adolescents during this time. Aaron and his family found the strength within them and learned new coping skills along the way.

Jeffers 'did not do conflict' of any kind. Conflict is an unavoidable part of mature adult life. No one with a rational mindset chooses conflict, but some of use like Jeffers knew it was a reality and developed skills with which to address it and deal with a communication breakdown between 2 family members who he adored.

Being good at conflict resolution did not mean Jeffers liked it; it probably meant he already had more than his fair share and he had to adapt to survive so that is where his conflict resolution skills came from. How then, did Jeffers turn a difficult moment within his family life into an opportunity to build rapport with the people that were dearest to him?

Win-Win was the style Jeffers used as a person who held a high concern for self and for others. Jeffers confronted the family broken relationship between his Aunty Claudia and grandfather, which had existed far too long. He used negotiation strategies to resolve them. He used the most constructive style of managing conflict – his aim was to bring about decisions and solutions which satisfied the family members involved.

Jeffers, the Win-Win negotiator recognised the importance his Aunty Claudia and grandfather attached to their needs, and he was not totally pre-occupied with meeting his own needs but was prepared to try to understand what his individual family's needs were as well. Jeffers made certain that all views were heard. His commitment to finding solutions was acceptable to those involved, as well as his sensitivity, belief in his family members and objectivity made him a constructive family member.

Today, Claudia and Cephas have rekindled their relationship under Aaron's direction, which was for his grandfather to initiate contact with his daughter shortly before he took ill. Jeffers taught these two loved ones how to communicate again and practice forgiveness.

Below is a heartfelt message from Cephas, Aaron's Grandfather to his beloved Grandson:

"Aaron was my grandson. He had a very bright future ahead of him as a young man. He was a friend to many and was well liked by all that knew him. My dear grandson was a sensitive young man, who always made time to visit me. On his arrival he would greet me with "Hello Grandad, how are you doing? I have come for a catch-up." We would carry on our conversations from where we had left off from his last visit.

Aaron's passing has left a deep hole in my heart that can never be filled. I often reflect on so many precious moments we had shared together. Each day I realise his dreams and ambitions, which were many, have not been fulfilled and nor will I see him fully mature into the amazing man I know he would have been. This indeed saddens my heart knowing how much he loved life. May you RIEP Aaron. I love you always." – Grandad Lescott. xx

Despite the backlash from the impact of a broken family relationship, sickness and death in the family, Aaron managed to continue to relish some popularity as an Amateur Footballer. Who would have thought watching, supporting and cheering Aaron on during numerous football practices and matches at George Dixon International School, where he attended as a secondary school student that this would have inspired him to go on and become a football superstar showcasing his football skills and talents when representing his employer, ASDA Perry Barr at their Sunday League matches regularly scoring superb goals.

Last Birthday Celebration

Birthdays are a great time for families to focus attention, encouragement and blessings on one person. Establishing traditions is important. Traditions give stability and joy as we anticipate and participate in experiences that bond us as families and create cherished memories.

On 29th September 2013, Joy had planned to be with her sons, Aaron and Kwayme and a few local neighbours throughout the day to celebrate Jeffers' 23rd birthday, without his knowledge.

For her son, Joy found some sweet and simple birthday celebrations that did not break the bank. Even though the family loved the big party celebrations, they still established family birthday traditions.

Over the years, Jeffers' mother has had the joy of watching Aaron grow up and catch the birthday spirit. In the early days, it was all her. She would second guess herself and wonder if she was depriving her children of the big birthdays their friends had. But on that day, she was quite sure that Aaron had already developed a deeper understanding of honouring a person and being content to keep the celebration simple.

My Son Dies, My Grandson Is Born

Everything started when 'baby bump's' mother was about 3 months pregnant in 2013; that was when 'baby bump' began to kick in the womb. 'Baby Bump' was the nickname that Jeffers and the mother of his child named their son, prior to him being born.

Jeffers announced to his family officially that he was going to be a dad. This was a precious blessing from Jehovah God, and the family happily granted him with their blessings.

Daddy Jeffers' shared joy of being a father was demonstrated with sheer excitement and his endless cute chatter with 'baby bump'; toys for 2, because it meant that he would be down with playing just a little bit with those genuinely cool toys his son received as gifts, and he got to play with them first – the young dad loved them as he bought his son stimulating baby toys himself; all swagged out with a great selection of Converse All Stars baby boy trainers in all different shades, colours and coolest designs.

The favourite part of Jeffers wanting to become a father was being able to watch his son growing up. He would have loved to watch him maturing and being able to experience his son's personality shaping and growing, hence seeing the creativity in all his child did. Being a part of that process would have been one of Jeffers' favourite things.

In 2014, Jeffers' son, a beautiful bundle of joy came into this world. On 13ᵗʰ March 2014, just 2 weeks before the birth of his child, Jeffers left it.

"Your stunning son talks about you. He visits you at your resting place and puts beautiful flowers all around you. We show him photos of you so that he knows what you look like and who you are. He is very funny, trendy, clever and chatty just like you. I have discovered that he also loves basketball and is very sporty. He also enjoys the outdoors and reciprocates those 3 important words I LOVE YOU - backing those words up with lots of hugs and kisses," Joy commented.

The Day My Son Died

"Sitting here watching TV, I cried my eyes out this evening (25th October 2019) and was reminded by Sinead Tinker (Katie McGlynn)'s heart-breaking terminal cancer storyline on 'Coronation Street', as she learns that her cancer is so far advanced, she has only weeks to live - how short life can be? This always makes me feel sad — it takes me back to the day my family and I lost a wonderful son, grandson, father, nephew — Aaron. He was not diagnosed or suffered with cancer, however Sinead's experience reminded me to always be grateful for what my family and I still have and for how far we have all come," wrote Joy.

For those of you who do not know Joy, her incredible son suffered two cardiac arrests 6 years ago, aged just 23. He was in a coma for nearly 2 weeks and had suffered a brain injury as a result of a lack of oxygen to his brain.

Joy added: *"This is my first ever book I have written, and I am a little unsure of how to write but here it goes! Let me just give you some background. My family is my world. My family was perfect — I am the mother to my 2 very good-looking princes Aaron and my second born, Kwayme now 15 years old, and me Joy — I loved my life! I worked full-time and around my handsome boys. Life was as most would think, perfect and we had our whole lives ahead of us, with everything to live for and look forward to. We were extremely excited about all the possibilities ahead."*

Aaron had no previous bouts of sickness and was a fit and healthy young man. He became unwell with a virus on 23rd October 2013, during his shift at ASDA Perry Barr and was rushed to hospital. He was hospitalised from late October 2013 and died at the Queen Elizabeth Hospital, Birmingham on the 13th March 2014.

It all began on the morning of 19th October 2013 when Aaron complained to his mother that he was feeling under the weather. Joy advised him to visit his local Health Centre for further investigation. When he returned from his local Health Centre, Joy called the paramedics to her home for further observation and tests as her son had collapsed to the ground complaining of intense and excruciating abdominal and back pain, which took his breath away. Morphine was administered to Aaron by the paramedics and a urine sample was taken. Paramedics concluded Aaron's urine was abnormal and he had a presumed urine infection. The paramedics drove Aaron to Good Hope Hospital Accident & Emergency Department in Birmingham. Antibiotics and painkillers were prescribed, and Aaron was advised to take the full course of medication prescribed. He was discharged from Good Hope Hospital on the evening of 19th October 2013.

On the evening of 24th October 2013, the paramedics were called to address Aaron's further complaint of abdominal and back pain, plus vomiting. Painkillers were administered by the paramedics and he was admitted to Sandwell General Hospital Accident & Emergency Hospital, Birmingham.

Aaron had a urinary catheter inserted on admission to the hospital. He soon developed an infection, caused by the trauma of the catheter been fitted. If you have ever had a urinary catheter, you will know that they are very unpleasant. If you have not, imagine someone threading a tube up through your urethra into your bladder and ... yes, yes, they hurt. Aaron was reviewed by a Consultant Urologist on the 25th October 2013, as further tests indicated Aaron's infection had worsened.

Further investigation suggested Aaron's prostate gland was infected (prostatitis). Joy remembers Aaron screaming out and crying like a baby on several occasions and how he became extremely afraid every time he had the urge to urinate. Aaron described this experience as *'feeling like cutting glass'*. Ladies ..... for those of you who have ever experienced or suffered with cystitis - pain, burning or stinging sensations when peeing you will have some understanding of the type of pain Aaron was under. Joy and members of her family would observe him request that his curtains be drawn around his bed. AJ would then place his dressing gown in his mouth to avoid patients on his ward hear his unbearable cries of pain, whilst holding onto his dear mother and family for their support, understanding and comfort.

It was evident on the 4th November 2013 that Aaron was seriously ill, not able to walk due to swelling to his entire body, and he was in a lot of pain. Aaron was needle phobic and feared receiving various types of injections and having blood samples withdrawn. For needle or injection phobic sufferers, they can experience temporary palpitations and increased heart rate or blood pressure. Their fear may also be expressed with increased blood pressure, shortness of breath, dry mouth, nausea, tremor, feeling faint or actually fainting, and/or feelings of panic. Needle or injection phobic sufferers may find it hard to watch or look at their blood, and/or to receive an injection or other medical procedure. They may avoid any medical contact for fear of being confronted by needles or injections. In experiencing a rush of fear the sufferer might find frightening thoughts running through their mind. These could be fears about losing control and/or that they are going to faint. They may have the thought that something bad is going to happen, even if they do not know what it is.

Aaron was discharged from Sandwell General Hospital on the 8th November 2013, with swelling to his body, and experienced difficulty in walking, and as a result was escorted to the car in a wheelchair. He was advised to complete the full 4 day course of antibiotics.

Aaron was re-admitted to Sandwell General Hospital on the 11th November 2013, and then discharged again the day after with swelling to his body and difficulty walking. Antibiotics were administered by the hospital.

"Aaron, I am reminded of the hospital journeys that I made to Sandwell General Hospital, Birmingham since your death, each time I drive past the hospital. I also remember when I used to come and see you as a patient there - the conversations that disclosed bad news; the procedures and pain you suffered; the hospital blunders; stress; expensive car parking and sometimes not able to find parking spaces. Memories still flood back over and over after 6 years. This makes me feel sad," Joy recalls.

Aaron received a telephone call from the Out Of Hours Badger Service on the evening of 21st November 2013, requesting him to get himself to Sandwell General Hospital Accident & Emergency Department as a matter of urgency.

This was to re-take his blood test as the blood results taken earlier that morning flagged up that his potassium level was too high. Aaron was not a happy man – he was very upset; in tears crying; anxious; unbelievably angry and frustrated that he had to go back to the hospital. Aaron's potassium was tested again, and was still high – his body was still infected, and he had a urine/protein infection plus a temperature which was treated with antibiotics.

What follows is a series of intimate text messages, which Jeffers sent to his mother during 22nd – 24th November 2013:

"Need to see you quickly." Time: 17.04 pm.

"Just want to see you, want to come home." Time: 17.08 pm.

"Miss you guys." Time: 20.47 pm.

"When will I be home? Sick of this place and feeling depressed." Time: 21.03 pm.

"Trust and faith has gone." Time: 21.12 pm.

"This place has killed the fight in me." Time: 21.36 pm.

"Thanks for your support." Time: 22.48 pm.

"Love you mom." Time: 23.20 pm.

"Thanks for lifting my spirits tonight, love u always." Time: 20.23 pm.

"Thanks for the support today, really lifted my spirits. "Time: 21.01 pm.

"Can't wait to see u tomorrow. "Time: 21.03 pm.

"Trying to remain positive for the day I can come out. Need to get better and stronger to be the old Aaron again." Time: 20.11 pm.

"Will u pray for me too?" Time: 20.14 pm.

"Love you so much mom." Time: 21.02 pm.

"Next destination is home." Time: 21.04 pm.

On the 28th November 2013, doctors had to perform a medical procedure, which Aaron was dreading due to his needle and injection phobia. In a text message, he wrote to his mother that evening:

"Could not have done it without you." Time: 23.45 pm.

The following morning, Aaron wrote in a text message to his mother:

"Thanks for last night and the support u gave." Time: 09.56 am. "Feel better and cannot wait to get out of here." Time: 09.57 am.

Throughout Aaron's stay at Sandwell General Hospital, Joy and her family witnessed him losing his pride, belief, determination, independence, confidence, self-respect and dignity. The family witnessed Aaron being extremely ill, afraid, fatigued, exhausted, stressed, frightened, demoralised and weak on the 2nd December

2013. Joy began to fear for her son's life and stayed with him for hours on end whilst in the care of Sandwell General Hospital, as she watched her son suffer discomfort, feeling helpless and unable to help him.

On the 2nd December 2013, doctors had to perform another medical procedure, which Aaron was not looking forward to because of his needle and injection phobia. In a text message to his mother, he wrote:

"Come earlier if you can, need support, son." Time: *16.38 pm.*

Aaron was later transferred to Queen Elizabeth Hospital, Birmingham on the 6th December 2013 with the support of his mother and a medical professional within Sandwell General Hospital. Aaron was put on a strict water reduction due to the swelling in his body. Joy wrote:

"His abdomen was so distended that he looked like he was in his 3rd trimester."

Over the next couple of days, fluid was drained from Aaron's body using the kidney dialysis machine.

On this day, the 9th December 2013, in a text message to his mother Aaron wrote:

"Need more fluid drained, come ASAP." Time: *10.01 am.*

During the day Aaron was feeling very anxious and frightened because a third medical procedure needed to be performed. He was given oxygen throughout the day to help him breathe properly. During the hospital visit, Aaron mentioned to his mother that he had not met the nurse standing opposite his bed administering medication to other patients on Aaron's ward. Joy encouraged her son to ascertain her name and stressed how important it was to find out just in case he needed her help. So, Aaron called her over to his bedside and introduced himself before asking the nurse her name.

Before leaving the hospital visit, Aaron expressed to his mother, Kwayme and Aunty Linda that his feet and hands were cold and requested his mother to rub those parts of his body that were cold to provide him with warmth. Little did his family know that his body was going in to septic shock. He also asked Joy, Kwayme, Aunty Linda and Nurse Jo that evening to pray for him. Nurse Jo explained that she was not a religious person, and that she had to administer mediation to the patients, however thanked Aaron for asking her. Aaron's wish was granted and a verse from the Psalms was read to him. Aaron, Joy, Kwayme and Aunty Linda all expressed those 3 important words *'I love you'* to one another before departing. Aaron's last spoken words to his dear mother; Kwayme and Aunty Linda was *"I love you guys"* whilst holding his fists firmly squeezed, emphasing his undying love for his family.

Shortly after departing, Aaron asked Nurse Jo in his care whether he was going to die. Aaron also questioned Joy and other family members whether he was going to die. That conversation was a very difficult one Joy had with Aaron. Hearing Aaron talk about the possibility that he might die was too much for Joy to stomach.

Excited Joy and Kwayme would see each other the following day, hopefully the next evening Aaron would spend time with his family members and friends once again. He would have! His mother, family and friends never would have guessed that a few hours later, it would be the start of their worst nightmare.

Every waking moment Joy replays that moment repeatedly in her mind, when the medical team at the Queen Elizabeth Hospital under Aaron's care informed her at 3:30 a.m. on the 10th December 2013, the following morning that Aaron had taken a turn for the worse after his mother and family members had left the hospital the night before.

Joy explains: *"It was 3:30 a.m. and my phone rang which made me jump out of my sleep. I saw the name 'QE Hospital' flash up on my landline phone display screen – totally oblivious about what I was about to hear. It was a call that would be the start of what was to be a huge change in me and my family's world. A change nothing can ever prepare you for.*

I answered, 'Hello,' and Nurse Jo said, 'Am I speaking to the mother of Aaron Jeffers?' to which I replied, "Yes."

"That phone call. I still shudder as to what happened that evening after I had left the hospital to visit my extremely sick son, and how the day that had only just started would unfold right in front of me and I would remain totally helpless and unable to do a single thing to help my phenomenal young man," Joy wrote.

Nurse Jo - *"Hi Joy, I do not want to alarm you. Aaron was doing so well after your visit to the hospital last night, but he has suffered two cardiac arrests."*

Me – *"No, No, No! What! Is he ok? Is he breathing and has he come around?"*

Nurse Jo – *"We have managed to get him back. Can you get yourself to the Queen Elizabeth Hospital as quickly as you can?"*

I knew the news I had just received was not good – my mind wanted to reach my son. I needed to get to him immediately! I called my sister, Claudia, and updated her on Aaron's situation and asked her to meet me at the hospital. He was at least 45 minutes away and I was a trembling wreck! I woke up Aaron's younger brother, Kwayme and explained we needed to go back to hospital to see his sick brother. My sister called my parents once we had all arrived at the hospital.

That 45 minute drive to the Queen Elizabeth Hospital was the quickest journey of my life, all I could do was keep looking at my watch – it was a wonder I did not get stopped by the police for speeding.

I arrived at the hospital and ran in as fast as I could, not knowing what to expect – I was taken straight through to a ward in critical care where Aaron was surrounded by the medical team – he was charcoal grey in colour and lifeless, there were wires everywhere.

It is funny what you notice in situations you do not expect to find yourself in and are nowhere near prepared for! Yes, he was a charcoal grey colour but still my Aaron in my mind - I did not want to accept that was my Aaron lying lifeless in that bed. I told the medical team to take him away – he looked nothing like my Aaron – he looked lifeless. A handful of nurses came to console me and offered me a hot drink. He had no gown on and there were wires everywhere and the machines that were attached to him were bleeping. I just did not know what to do.

No one spoke at first but then the medical team just said, "this is his mother" and they stopped and stepped back – they had been waiting for me – I knew it, keeping him alive until I got there – what was I supposed to do now?

Then a voice, "Joy I am Dr ???" I cannot even remember the name of the doctor. "Aaron is very ill, all we know is his heart stopped – we do not know why.

There was a lack of oxygen going to his brain causing a brain injury – so we need to do a brain scan to see if any damage has been caused." I screamed in my mind and out loud, "What??" He is only 23! He is young and so fit! This cannot be happening to me!! I could not speak – I just stood there sobbing my heart out with all of these bizarre thoughts going around in my screaming head – I was so numb. I was in shock. My first born had died twice and was still dying.

I could hear him struggling to breathe – a crackling bubbling sound with every breath!

I put my face on the side of Aaron's face and put my mouth beside his ear. I cannot remember exactly what I said, but I told him that I loved him always and forever, and I told him his brother, Kwayme and family loved him too – I named them all individually so that maybe he could process it better through his unconscious state. I told him he was so strong and that he was a soldier and my hero.

I also told him he was an amazing son and that his family and I needed him. I begged him not to leave us – and I asked him not to give up without a fight. I kissed his face and held his hand. I turned to my sister in the waiting area, tears streaming down my face.

I knew that I needed to be strong for my younger boy, and I had to believe Aaron was going to be okay, and while he was still breathing with the support of the ventilator and thereafter went on to breathe by himself, I had hope – I had to hold on to that. In my mind – he was going to be okay!

Nurse Jo disclosed prior to Aaron's cardiac arrest (crash-landing), he called out her name "Nurse Jo", and she immediately came to his rescue. Nurse Jo later added "Aaron was unbelievably petrified and very anxious. His first born was due to be born in March 2014."

Aaron was put on life support, which was keeping him alive. He required life support/ventilator for his breathing. He was placed on a ventilator and other machines – wires coming from every direction because of medical problems which made it hard for him to breathe fully on his own. At one point his condition was so severe that the ventilator was used to totally breathe for him. His family never left his side. They took turns holding his hands while the ventilator pushed air in and out of his lungs. His body swelled from the flood of fluids and antibiotics. However, Aaron managed to pull through and began breathing on his own without any ventilators. *"It was like divine intervention taking place right in front of my eyes,"* Joy wrote.

Joy always re-assured Aaron that he would get better and that it was possible he would get through this. She was also so positive, and truly thought it was possible.

Jeffers slept a lot and his condition kept changing. He could not speak to anyone and developed collapsed lungs, needing to undergo a Tracheostomy procedure, as he was now a critical care patient.

Joy recalls asking herself how she could help Aaron and if there was something, she could do to make him feel better, although she knew he could not answer.

When someone is ill and cut off from their daily life, a visit, call or note from someone reminds them they are remembered, part of a community and are cared for. Joy's physical and emotional touch brought Aaron great comfort and whenever it seemed appropriate, she would give him a hug or extend a hand, touch him like she used to, pray with him, gently apply his favourite body cream to his body, hands, arms and feet. She played his best-loved soothing tunes from a dynamic range across music genres to help make him feel comfortable and accepted.

She can only imagine what Aaron must have been feeling inside. Illness carries with it a whole load of feelings: fear, anger, disappointment, hopelessness, sadness, grief, perhaps guilt or even shame.

Aaron was always excited to know his mother, family and friends were present by his bedside when they visited. The monitors would always beep when his mother, family or friends arrived to see him. It really lifted Aaron's spirits.

After a number of hospital procedures, Jeffers developed pneumonia and other complications, including problems with his chest and breathing.

Jeffers was also in distress. There were so many people in the room. Test results started coming back – the family did not even know everything. The mystery had just begun.

On the evening before Aaron's demise, his immediate family had visited him in hospital as normal. Aaron began to exhibit a change in his breathing pattern - breathing became rapid and regular. Lastly, his breathing became shallow, quiet, and began slowing down.

Medics use the phrase "lub-dub, lub-dub" to describe the sound the heart makes: this is what you can hear through a stethoscope. As Joy and her second born, Kwayme waited and before informing Aaron that they would see him again tomorrow, although not wanting to leave his side, Aaron looked straight into his mother's eyes as she could read his mind.

Joy recollects, *"It was as if Aaron was trying to tell me to stop explaining to him that she was going to take his brother Kwayme home to prepare him for school in the morning. I will never forget the look in his eyes. It was as if he was trying to hurry me up to leave. Aaron's reaction was something I had never seen before – it was out of character!"* Joy expressed to Aaron how much she loved him, and his brother informed him of the same before they departed that evening.

This was the last lucid moment Joy and her second born had with Aaron! On reflection, she believes Aaron knew what was coming and he did not want his mother or his brother to be present when it happened.

"In Aaron's eyes, Joy had witnessed; been through and seen enough pain. This was Aaron's way of trying to make it okay for her and his brother. Can you even imagine how difficult it was for Aaron in those last moments? The moment when he knew that not only his own life was about to end, but that he would never properly experience fatherhood or be able to raise his first born – a life he helped create? Can you imagine as a father knowing he could not grow with his son? Can you imagine Aaron watching his sweet child taking his first breath – taking his first steps, holding his first born for the first time, full of joyful emotion and telling his son how much he loves him as his life came to an end? As a parent and a mother, I can tell you, Aaron's greatest fear was realised today and it was not the fear of his own life, but that of his beautiful son. As a parent, your life means nothing in comparison to the lives of your children. We live for our children; we breathe for them – they are our reason for being. Just thinking of his internal struggle in those last moments rips my heart into pieces. He knew his young life was ending. He knew he was leaving precious siblings and family behind, not forgetting his child. Oh, how his heart must have ached. Can you even imagine the agony that played out in his mind? Every parents' worst nightmare happening to him in real time. And that is the only solace I can find in this – that Aaron is here in spirit and is here in his son's life watching over him to remind him of his undying love," Joy wrote.

Joy had just arrived home. At the point when Aaron's organs were shutting down, and the medical team had performed every medical intervention that they could, she was alerted by a family member during a telephone conversation to return to the hospital as quickly as she could - Aaron had taken a turn for the worse. On arriving to the hospital around 12:45 a.m. on the 13th March 2014, Joy was informed by medical staff in Aaron's care he had passed away at 12.05 a.m. The nurse greeted and came to see her in the waiting room. The nurse took Lescott off to a side room down the hall. Her face was blank. She knew she was about to get the news every parent feared! They sat down in a conference room. The nurse closed the door and asked if there was family they could call. Joy informed the nurse that her son's immediate family were already in the waiting room. Joy just wanted the update.

The nurse explained again the horrible findings/results. She added there was nothing the medical team could have done to save Aaron's life. Aaron's brain was injured from the lack of oxygen to his brain whilst suffering two cardiac arrests; Pneumonia; Castleman's Disease (medical terminology for multi-organ shutdown).

Prior to Aaron's decline, the medical team explained to Joy that even if he pulled through, the parts of him that made him Aaron would all be gone. Medics also informed Joy they did not expect Aaron to make it over and over, however Joy still had faith, hope and believed that her son would pull through; get up; crack jokes and walk out of that hospital, ready to come home.

In that moment, Joy, the mother of this fighting hero's heart broke! How was she supposed to accept that? How was she supposed to even think about life without her special young man? It was not fair!

The medical team told the family they could go back to the room where Aaron lay peacefully resting. His family waiting in the waiting room could not get to him fast enough. Everyone came into the room to pay their last personal respects.

It was so hard to leave Aaron at the hospital, alone. The only reason Joy did this is because she knew her son understood that she had a younger sibling to take care of. Aaron would have told his mother to leave him and go home to her younger son. So, she did. That moment she went back into the waiting room where the rest of the family were waiting. Kwayme (then 9 years old) said out loud:

"Aaron is lying in bed looking at the clock."

Everyone in the waiting area began looking at each other. A family member whispered in Joy's ear:

"Kwayme does not know does he?"

Joy was in utter shock and overlooked to tell her son of the shocking and devastating news. In her mind, this devastating news had to come from her and only her – she was the only person to tell her second born.

In a quiet area in the hospital, Joy explained to her 9-year-old child what had happened with great thought, care and sensitivity in the form of a short story in a child friendly way:

"Aaron wishes he could still walk, talk and joke with you, the family and his friends, but he knew that he could not. Your brother was very sick, and his body stopped working. He cannot come back to life, even though we so desperately want him to.

To help explain, imagine a living leaf on a tree, then when it falls to the ground it dies - all beautiful living things have a beginning and eventually have an end. As time goes by, you will remember special things your brother taught you to do, and you will take great comfort in the happy times you both spent with your brother. Remember, Aaron loves you always and forever."

They both held each other tight and cried their eyes out together in that moment.

Joy remembers consciously watching Aaron in the bed. She wanted to see him get up out of his sleep and see him breathe, smile, walk, laugh and affectionately hug her.

"It felt like a dream. It was something I will never forget," wrote Joy. Then she just held him, stroked his face and held his hand.

On 13th March 2014, Jeffers died, and his mother's life changed forever – the worst days of her life. From that moment forward, it seems the question Joy kept asking herself was *"What do I do now?"* She is not sure if that will ever change.

"It was so incredibly hard for me to leave the room and hospital that morning," Joy wrote.

"This morning I am overwhelmingly heartbroken. I am kissing one less head good morning. Tonight, I will be crawling into bed feeling immense pain instead of feeling extremely happy from the warm embrace of my first born's hugs which made me feel acknowledged, gave me great comfort and re-assured me everything was going to be okay each night before going to bed. Tomorrow morning, I will wake to realise it was not all a dream and peel myself out of my bed to be there for my second born. My second born has no brother to share his life with and no brother to tell him how proud he is of him. With my broken heart I will wipe

away tears and say it will all be okay. I will make one less breakfast, do less dishes and laundry - all the things that I will wish for a chance to do all over again. With this realisation, isn't it scary knowing that any time could be the last you talk to someone? ALWAYS tell the people who care about you and who are important to you how much you truly love them each and every day. Do not save it for tomorrow because tomorrow may be too late," Joy added.

Knowing she was leaving her beloved first-born son lying in that bed. She was never going to physically see him, feel him, and touch him again. It just felt so final.

"You were so amazingly strong son, how you dealt with everything that was thrown at you whilst in hospital," stated Joy.

The hardest thing Joy has ever had to hear is that her first born child is no longer on this earth; however, Aaron is in Jehovah God's memory and remains in her heart forever.

The hardest thing she will ever have to do is to live every day since that moment of loss. How do you move on from losing a child? Everything she does is done because she thinks *"What would Aaron want/do?"*

Two years later, Joy and her family were informed by Sandwell & West Birmingham Hospital NHS Trust at a Resolution Meeting held on 24th April 2016 that during the 7 weeks whilst in their care they did not have any diagnosis for Aaron's symptoms.

The diagnosis was hard to pinpoint. It was during this meeting, that it was disclosed Aaron's symptoms on admission in October 2013 was Sepsis.

Doctors diagnosed Sepsis in Aaron using several physical findings such as: fever, low blood pressure, increased heart rate and difficulty in breathing. It was a brutal death for such a beautiful person. The doctors and nurses treated Aaron's Sepsis with antibiotics; he received oxygen and intravenous IV fluids to maintain blood flow and oxygen to his organs; given kidney dialysis and assisted his breathing with a machine.

Sepsis

Sepsis is the result of a massive immune response to bacterial infection that gets into the blood. Any bodily infection can trigger the condition of the lungs; urinary tract and abdominal area are particularly susceptible. The body releases immune chemicals into the blood to combat the infection.

Those chemicals trigger widespread inflammation, which leads to blood clots and leaky blood vessels. It often leads to organ failure or injury. Sepsis is a medical emergency that become fatal or life changing for many individuals who develop this blood poisoning, called Septicaemia. Many of the signs and symptoms of Sepsis, such as fever and difficulty breathing, are the same as in other conditions, making sepsis hard to diagnose in its early stages.

With a rise in Sepsis deaths, Joy is reminded that more must be done to educate families, nurses, and doctors to recognise the early signs of Sepsis so that patients do not have to continue to suffer what her son did.

With all the advances in medicine, there still seems to be ignorance and neglect around Sepsis; yes, neglect.

If there is anything that Joy has taken from this devastating experience, it is knowledge.

"If I knew then what I know now, I would not be writing this book. Always identify someone who can accompany you or your loved one to act as an Advocate. Ask questions, demand answers. If you do not get any answers, seek other opinions. Learn the symptoms of Sepsis. Flu-like symptoms, fevers, low body temperature, extreme lethargy, inability to urinate.

Learn what tests can better indicate Sepsis. CBC (complete blood count) with differential, which gives readings of white blood cell counts and red blood cell counts, platelets and haemoglobin. Learn the names of certain germs and terms that are linked to Sepsis – VRE (Vancomycin- resistant Enterococcus), E. coli, pseudomonas aeruginosa, klebsiella, MRSA (methicillin-resistant Staphylococcus aureus) and necrotizing fasciitis.

If you think you or a loved one has the symptoms of Sepsis, call 999 or go to your local Accident & Emergency Hospital immediately. Trust your instincts."

Castleman's Disease

Castleman's disease is a group of rare disorders characterised by lymph node enlargement, specific microscopic changes to the lymph nodes, and a broad range of symptoms and laboratory findings.

The lymph nodes, and the cells that reside in them (lymphocytes), are an integral part of our immune system that help us fight invading organisms. For reasons unknown, these lymph nodes undergo some transformations that result in overproduction of lymphocytes and other inflammatory compounds.

On 9th January 2016, Joy came across an excellent website www.cdcn.org for support and information about Castleman's Disease. At that time, it was impossible for her to focus on anything, 2 years after losing her loved one to the illness. She was distracted by memories of her son.

"Today, 14th March 2020 I wrote on Castleman's Disease Collaborative Network's website: I wish I would have known about this website back in 2014 when my 23 year old son died from this terrible infection. This is a great site full of support, resources and information that people need to be aware of in order to raise awareness amongst their loved ones. Keep up the good work and research in order to help find a cure for those diagnosed with Castleman's.

David Fajgenbaum, Founder of the Castleman's Disease Collaborative Network and Physician-Researcher studying Castleman's Disease replied and wrote on the 19th March 2020: *Hi Joy, I am so sorry to see about you losing your son to Castleman's Disease in 2014 from your post on the CDCN page. I also have Castleman's Disease and nearly died 5 times since I became ill 5 years ago and I research Castleman's Disease to get us closer to a cure for people like your son. If you would like to help fight against Castleman's Disease, you can take 15-20 minutes to enrol your son into our registry at www.cdcn.org/accelerate. Thanks so much for considering this. I would like to help you with looking into whether your son died from Castleman's Disease. Let me know if you have any questions. All my best, David.*

On 19th March 2020, I responded to Physician-Researcher: *Hi David, I will consider helping with the fight against Castleman's Disease by joining the ACCELERATE Register. I am very proud of what you are doing to try and find a cure for people like my son. Best wishes Joy."*

Joy encourages you and your loved ones to utilise the CDCN site to educate yourselves about this horrible disease to become aware of it in order to help solve this serious problem amongst humanity.

Wishes For My Grandson

When asked for the best thing about having grandchildren, grandparents talk about the joys of loving and being loved, watching grandchildren grow, and seeing themselves live on through their grandchildren.

One of the things Joy notices with her grandchild is the joy that he brings. He has shown a great deal of interest in what Joy is doing and how she is. It is just lovely having grandchildren who are really interested in you and concerned about you. When you enjoy your time together remember that while you are playing and having fun with your grandchildren, you are also helping their development and nurturing your relationship. The relationship between grandparents and grandchildren, is unique, there is nothing quite like it. It benefits both generations in so many ways. Grandchildren love to hear about their family history, all those amazing characters that all families have. Grandparents give the grandchildren all the time they want, because they can. It is these sorts of things that grandparents and extended family members miss beyond words when contact is not there. As we all know from estranged grandchildren, they miss all of that as well, and they keep those memories forever.

Joy believes if you are fortunate enough to have grandchildren near you, they keep you young, because there is always something happening.

Joy added: *"Aaron's sickness and sudden passing, has allowed me to start thinking about my grandson's future since he has gone.*

"I would like you, my darling grandson to love music because it makes us feel good. Music provides us with feelings of joy and pleasure and is a strong form of expression. Through music, many emotions can be shown whether that be happy, sad, or angry. Enjoy football and basketball just like your father did because rooting for sports teams and athletes provides a sense of belonging and will also bolster your self-esteem. Sport will develop your sense of friendliness and develop your team spirit. It will also help you develop mental and physical toughness.

Strive for excellence = being outstanding, achieving greatness, brilliance and distinction to achieve your dreams and goals. Carry on living your father's legacy – love life. We have been given the gift of life. Once we love our lives, we will then set big goals to make the most of the limited time we have to make an impact. So, appreciate your life and love life for what it is.

The gift of life is something to be appreciated and treasured. Once you love your life you need to be totally enthusiastic and excited about your life. Just think of it as an opportunity to experience this world as it is. If we want to experience all the beauty that life has to offer, we need to be enthusiastic about life despite the obstacles each one of us face. Be grateful always, because your attitude towards everything in your life will play a greater role going forward. Your attitude will be reflected in the way other people treat you. Maintaining an upbeat attitude will attract abundance and joy in your life. When you are totally grateful about your life you experience joy. Self-accept yourself because you are totally unique in this world. This means no one else can be you and you cannot be anyone else. Be totally comfortable with who you are as a person – love thy self. Accept everything about yourself and change what you want to. No one else can bring the talent you were born with. Your talent must be brought out only by you. So, tap into your amazing strengths and bring out your talent. Find work that you love. Work is going to fill a large part of your life and finding work that we really love is one of the key decisions we can make in our lives. Find a cause that you are so passionate about because we are only here for a short or limited time, so find the work that invigorates you. Once you find your main cause, you will be living your legacy just like your daddy did. Trust in relationships is built on a foundation of truth. When you always tell the truth, you feel great about yourself and everyone around you will understand that you mean business. People always respond favourably to those who live by and speak their truth. At the end of your life what will be important is that you lived your life according to your character and values. Keep aligning all your actions to what you want your life to stand for. This action will ensure you will live your legacy. Inspiring others is one the keys to leaving a legacy. If you ever become a Leader, you will need to inspire others to bring out their best selves. Even in your own family you can inspire your children through your actions. So always set a great example which will inspire everyone around you. Inspiring others to achieve their goals will help you leave a legacy. Respect everyone always, irrespective of their position or financial status. When you respect everyone, you feel a lot better about yourself. Respect others for who they are and what they stand for. Again, leaving a legacy can only happen if people understand that you value them. We are all deserving of success - all of us have the same opportunity as anyone else to achieve what we want. Some of us will start further behind than others, but that time can be made up with learning and working hard. Live a legacy grandson, as well as leave it!"

It is too painful for me to contemplate, but important that I express what I would like for you, my dear grandson."

It has been impossible not to put ourselves in the position of Aaron, a young man who was very much looking forward to becoming a father for the first time, only to have it torn apart and replaced with fear, uncertainty and the emptiness of knowing he would not see his baby boy grow up. Or the position of Joy, trying to stay strong and trying to hold it together while watching her first born fade away, robbed of precious years and decades of family joy, hardships and journeys faced with a future of uncertainty and loss. Or indeed the position of the relatives around our lost loved ones, somewhere we have all been – after all, is there anyone who has not endured the loss of someone they love?

For practical and emotional support at the end of life and through bereavement visit:

www.macmillan.org.uk

www.cruse.org.uk

www.childbereavementuk.org

www.gingerbread.org.uk

www.cclg.org.uk

www.bereavementadvice.org

This story is one of love and courage, life and death, highs and lows and above all determination, hope and faith.

"I will now continue to complete the later chapters of this book about my Aaron, my family, our struggles as we continue to learn to live again. I am mother, sister, aunty and me trying to hold it together without a guidebook to help me. This is my journey," Joy wrote.

Eternal Love: Mother's Love

"Of all the types of love, my love for you Aaron is the strongest. The love between you and I rose instantly, as a bond uniting two bodies and souls. My love for you is unconditional and eternal.

We formed a very strong bond of attachment that I will never ever forget, from the day you were born, building a very tight relationship which affected the way you related to others throughout your lifetime.

I offered you, my first-born unconditional love even before you were born because you were a part of me, and filled a gap I never knew existed, flooding me with tenderness and fragility.

When I took on the role of motherhood, I revealed a new part of myself. I became stronger, capable of sacrificing everything for you. I feed, protected and cared for you until you could take on life on your own.

We had many many many moments of affectionate, warm and happy times, but *there were also feelings of anger, frustration, and loss of patience.*

With perseverance and unconditional love, I can now see that you reaped the benefits for the rest of your life!

Thank you for all the lovely verbal expressions of your love for me, affectionate hugs, birthday and mothers' day cards/gift and best wishes you wrote to me.

I guess this was your way of expressing and demonstrating to me how appreciative you were of me during your 23 years, 6 months on this planet. Love you endlessly — mom xx"

Aaron wrote:

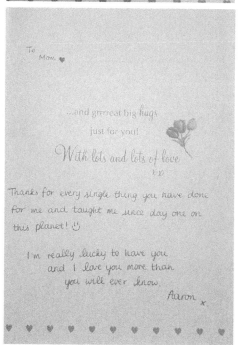

Mum
From Both of Us

To
Joy Maxine Lescott (Best Mom In The World)

THANKS FOR ALWAYS BEING
SUCH A SPECIAL MUM,
EVERY DAY OF THE YEAR

HAPPY MOTHER'S DAY
WITH LOVE FROM BOTH OF US

Love You Forever, God blessed us with you
Aaron & Kwayne

18.3.12
x

"People warned me that Mother's Day would be hard Aaron. Each year I display and read your handwritten messages, kissing each card. I loved the greeting cards you chose for me - pops of pink and colourful flowers.

You and Kwayme are the anchors of my life. I miss the many ways you would surprise and delight me, making Mother's Day one to remember with your lovely range of gifts," said Joy.

Funeral Home Gave Family Precious Time

The family was required to transfer Aaron from the Queen Elizabeth Hospital where he sadly passed away. For those few days, Aaron's family came to visit him at a local funeral home before the funeral, to just hold, cuddle him and pay their last respects.

Those few days helped the family come to terms with what had happened. It sounds silly but being able to go over to him and give him a kiss and cuddle – and just physically touch him gave his mother some relief. Joy cannot thank the funeral home enough for offering this facility.

As a parent, it is the worst thing to imagine your child in a morgue surrounded by death. This facility meant he had his own room where the family could see him whenever they wanted to. It also gave the family the opportunity to put his favourite songs on and talk to him. Jeffers' mother came to realise that those few days following the death of her son was so important and keeping him physically around helped her to adjust to the new situation. It was a huge comfort to have Aaron's calm presence in the room with his family, and by the time the family had to say their final farewells they knew they had some incredible memories to take with them.

Tragic Death & Untimely Passing

Aaron, who was thought to be a 'champion' of ASDA Perry Barr's Self-Scan Checkouts died at the tender age of just 23 on the 13th March 2014. The father of one passed away just five months after falling ill, having celebrated his 23rd birthday in the presence of his family and friends on 29th September 2013. He is survived by his parents, two brothers, sister and son.

The young father sadly passed away two weeks before his son was born in 2014. He told everyone he could not wait to become a father and was so excited about the imminent birth of his first child.

News of his death was announced on Facebook, within the ASDA Perry Barr Store, Birmingham and featured in the *Sunday Mercury* newspaper dated 3rd January 2016.

For Joy, each moment felt obscure. She felt lost, alone, empty and the disbelief was so intense immediately after Aaron's death. Her world was falling apart around her, and she did not know what to do. She was in utter shock, and it would take her a long time to grasp what had happened. It was hard for her to believe that someone as important as her first born was not coming back. Joy felt disorientated - as if she had lost her place and purpose in life. Feelings of pain and distress following her son's bereavement proved overwhelming and very frightening to Joy. She felt angry because Aaron's death seemed so cruel and unfair, especially when she felt Aaron died before his time and he had plans for his future. Joy's life felt like it no longer held any meaning. She longed for her son – seeing Aaron and hearing his voice. That was her brain's way of trying to process his death and acknowledge the finality of it. Joy's life would never be the same again.

Death Certificate

Joy collected Aaron's medical certificate from Queen Elizabeth Hospital, signed by the doctor who was responsible for Aaron when he died. The same doctor handed Joy her son's death certificate and was advised to read it carefully. She thanked the doctor and his team for everything they did for Aaron.

One of the most harrowing things Joy had to then deal with following the loss of Aaron was registering his death at the Birmingham Registry Office before his burial could go ahead. Joy needed to complete this legal requirement within 5 days of Aaron's death.

Joy recalls *"When I saw the Registrar, she was very empathetic towards me during the registering of Aaron's death. She was professional in her approach and shook my hand on arrival, whilst offering her sincere condolences. How was it even possible that both I and the mother of Aaron's child was sitting in a room with The Registrar just a few days after Aaron had passed away?*

It was so distressing having to provide this lady with Aaron's personal information and hand over all of the required paperwork, as well as communicate with her about something so sad whilst tears were pouring down my face. I did not want to be there, but I needed to witness the legalities of this legal process being signed off. It was at this point, that hard reality of my grandson, growing up without his father kicked in. There was my grandson sitting beside me, only a few weeks old without a father. It is sad to think that he will not be celebrating Father's Day in person with Aaron because he is deceased. Instead, my grandson will bring his father flowers at his grave.

My thoughts took me back to when I registered your birth and I was exceedingly happy – a beautiful baby boy. Little did I know then that 23 years and 6 months later I would be registering your death.

When the Registrar had all the information that she needed and entered Aaron's death in the register, she handed me Aaron's death certificate to give to Goodridge-Milford Funeral Directors. I did not want to arrange a funeral at what was already a difficult time. I found it baffling, terrifying, weird, overwhelming and devastating – a very complex mixture of feelings and emotions.

It all started with Goodridge-Milford Funeral Directors. They moved Aaron's body without any fuss and handed over the paperwork. The first meeting with Goodridge-Milford Funeral Directors took forever - ticking off the first 100 of those 1,000 decisions that needed to be made. Where do you want the service; what time should the funeral be; how many cars; cremation or burial; pine or oak; chrome handles or gold-painted ones; live music or taped; will anyone be visiting the body; do you want the corpse to have makeup, etc etc. The family had to make up the answers on the spot, as though we had an opinion.

All this at a time when we were feeling that our whole world had ended, and I no longer actually existed."

Funeral Of Aaron Jeffers

Organising a child's funeral is a job for which no parent can be prepared. The death of your child is perhaps the most painful thing that has ever happened to you and your family and this may be the first time you have been involved in making funeral arrangements. The funeral is the last physical act of caring for your child. It is a time, surrounded by profound grief, when you can acknowledge your child and the meaning your child's life holds for you and your family.

Joy wrote: *"Arranging Aaron's funeral seemed so unreal. It was probably the most difficult task I had to face. I had never planned a funeral before in my life.*

I have attended funerals in the past, but now I am faced with the overwhelming task of planning something loving and meaningful for Aaron. How do I begin? What are my options? Do I have to use a traditional funeral home?

Arranging catering was extremely difficult, particularly when you have no idea how many people to cater for. How could my family and I arrange a funeral at such an arduous time?" Joy explained.

The postman delivered more sympathy cards. I smiled and thanked him on each day I greeted him as I collected the heap of cards off him. If only he knew they were condolence messages and kind gestures to help support me and my family through Aaron's loss!" Joy described.

The public funeral service of the late Aaron Jeffers started on 4th April 2014 at 10:00 am and was held at the George Street Baptist Church, Lozells, Birmingham.

"I am feeling totally lost and very sad today. I still cannot comprehend you will never be coming home again.

Family from London have come to see you today and I got dressed in your bedroom this morning, surrounded by all of your belongings trying to make sense of everything and nothing is making any sense. I have no words for the pain that I feel. How am I, Kwayme and the family going to get through the funeral?"

The coffin was escorted by Goodridge-Milford Funeral Directors from Aaron's family home.

The ceremony finished at Aaron's resting place in Witton Cemetery, Birmingham.

Over 1,000 people attended the ceremony in George Street Baptist Church.

Aaron's coffin, draped with a stunning sympathy spray with pink carnations was brought to the church by Goodridge-Milford Funeral Directors on the morning of his funeral.

Before the service commenced, two photos of Aaron were placed on top of his casket, either side of the sympathy spray.

The church ceremony at George Street Baptist Church opened at 10:00 am and lasted two hours.

Celebration

of

Aaron Silas Cephas Jeffers

Sunrise 29th September 1990 - Sunset 13th March 2014

Funeral Service will be held

on

Friday 4th April 2014 @ 10.00 am

New Testament Church of God
240- 244 Lozells Road
Handsworth
Birmingham
B19 1NP

Interment at 1.00pm
Witton Cemetery
Moor Lane
Witton
Birmingham
B6 7AE

Officiating Minister:
Reverend Mike Harmon

There were so many people outside the church and twice as much inside the church. So many people wanted to come up and hug the bereaved family of Aaron. So many young people in church – WOW.

On arrival in to the church, the family was guided by Goodridge-Milford Funeral Directors into position. Ten pallbearers, who were selected by family members helped to carry Aaron's casket inside the church and to the burial site at the funeral, directed by Goodridge-Milford Funeral Directors.

Six of the pallbearers were dressed in red snapback hats and red t-shirts with Aaron's nicknames printed on the front: 'Jeffers', 'Mimic', 'Mr Jeffers', 'Aaron', 'AJ' and 'AJizay (Xbox nickname)' and his picture on the back, artistically designed by Aaron's cousin Shanai. The colour theme of the funeral was based on Aaron's favourite colour (red).

Joy held her head up high, as she walked behind the coffin next to Kwayme, her second-born, her grandson, his mother and her daughter. The rest of the family also walked behind Aaron's coffin into the church.

There was a musical tribute played and dedicated to Aaron as he was musically inclined.

The local church played tribute songs for him as he entered and exited the church. Tribute songs: 'The Man' by Aloe Blacc (on arrival) and 'What A Wonderful World' – Louis Armstrong (leaving the church).

'The Man' Lyrics

"Well, you can tell everybody
Yeah, you can tell everybody
Go ahead and tell everybody
I'm the man, I'm the man, I'm the man

Yes I am, yes I am, yes I am
I'm the man, I'm the man, I'm the man
I believe every lie that I ever told
Paid for every heart that I ever stole

I played my cards and I didn't fold
Well it ain't that hard when you got soul
(This is my world)

Somewhere I heard that life is a test
I been through the worst but still, I give my best
God made my mold different from the rest
Then he broke that mold so I know I'm blessed
(This is my world)

Stand up now and face the sun
Won't hide my tail or turn and run
It's time to do what must be done
Be a king when kingdom comes

Well, you can tell everybody
Yeah, you can tell everybody
Go ahead and tell everybody
I'm the man, I'm the man, I'm the man

Yes I am, yes I am, yes I am
I'm the man, I'm the man, I'm the man

I got all the answers to your questions
I'll be the teacher you could be the lesson
I'll be the preacher you be the confession
I'll be the quick relief to all your stressing

(This is my world)

It's a thin line between love and hate
Is you really real or is you really fake
I'm a soldier standing on my feet
No surrender and I won't retreat
(This is my world)

Stand up now and face the sun
Won't hide my tail or turn and run
It's time to do what must be done
Be a king when kingdom comes

Well, you can tell everybody
Yeah, you can tell everybody
Go ahead and tell everybody
I'm the man, I'm the man, I'm the man
Well, you can tell everybody
Yeah, you can tell everybody
Go ahead and tell everybody
I'm the man, I'm the man, I'm the man
Well, you can tell everybody
Yeah, you can tell everybody
Go ahead and tell everybody
I'm the man, I'm the man, I'm the man

Yes I am, yes I am, yes I am
I'm the man, I'm the man, I'm the man
I'm the man
Go ahead and tell everybody what I'm saying y'all
I'm the man
Go ahead and tell everybody what I'm saying y'all

Well, you can tell everybody
Yeah, you can tell everybody
Go ahead and tell everybody
I'm the man, I'm the man, I'm the man
Well, you can tell everybody
Yeah, you can tell everybody

Go ahead and tell everybody
I'm the man, I'm the man, I'm the man
Well, you can tell everybody
Yeah, you can tell everybody
Go ahead and tell everybody
I'm the man, I'm the man, I'm the man

Yes I am, yes I am, yes I am
I'm the man, I'm the man, I'm the man."

'The Man', a swaggering can-do anthem is about believing in oneself. The song's music video revisits both some of the adversities that African Americans have had to overcome and a selection of their triumphs. The moral of this song is about being you. This means you like who you are. Being yourself means living life how you want to live it, regardless of other people's opinions. Being yourself means you respect yourself. Being yourself means not worrying about what others think – after all we cannot control them or their thoughts. Believing in yourself means to love yourself first (start from within), then everything else will fall into place. You can do anything you put your mind to – anything is possible with a positive mental attitude.

The less you love yourself, listen to yourself, and understand yourself, the more confused, angry, and frustrating your reality will be.

When you begin and continue to love yourself more, the more everything you see, everything you do, want, and everyone you interact with, will begin to manifest into your life.

'What A Wonderful World' Lyrics

"I see trees of green, red roses too
I see them bloom for me and you
And I think to myself what a wonderful world

I see skies of blue and clouds of white
The bright blessed day, the dark sacred night
And I think to myself what a wonderful world

The colours of the rainbow so pretty in the sky
Are also on the faces of people going by
I see friends shaking hands saying how do you do
They're really saying I love you

I hear babies crying, I watch them grow
They'll learn much more than I'll never know
And I think to myself what a wonderful world
Yes I think to myself what a wonderful world."

When Louis Armstrong wrote and recorded this song America was segregated and racial tensions were still running very high. Americans were also living their lives pretty much certain that a nuclear bomb was going to strike them at some point. Armstrong was the target of much hate.

His message was that despite everything going on around the world, there is so much beauty in this planet and so much hope for the children and their future. The whole point of the song is that no matter how bad things can be, just take a look around, admire the world for its natural beauty and never lose hope for a wonderful future. Armstrong was just simply appreciating the good things that were around him.

The church service opened with the traditional singing of 'All Things Bright & Beautiful', 'The Lord Is My Shepherd' and closed with 'Amazing Grace.'

During the service, each speaker, poet, singer shared a personal reminiscence about Aaron, some breaking down – this was to be expected as a way of a show of emotion to reveal how much they cherished him.

"Aaron, Simeon did you so, so proud on the day of your burial when reading out his heartfelt speech about you during the church service whilst dealing with his own grief of losing you. I need you to understand that even though you both had a disagreement shortly before you became unwell, I know deep down you both still had a very deep soul connection – a strong bond like no other. Simeon demonstrated this when he sat by your bedside in hospital on numerous occasions during your 5 months stay in hospital. I must say, Simeon took your loss very badly, like we all have. The family still feels it today. It sure was brotherly love between you both. Seems like Simeon followed your footsteps and fathered a

beautiful baby daughter, named Essence in April 2019 – a day I will never ever forget, because it has so much significance and reminds me of you."

A selection of prayers was read out in church to allow the bereaved to remember Aaron, wish him to find rest, peace and life thereafter, and to express a range of feelings.

At the ceremony, the coffin remained closed out of privacy and respect for Aaron. It was inappropriate and disrespectful to have opened it.

Having an open casket viewing would have been an invasion of Aaron's privacy. Joy knew it was not what Aaron would have wanted. It was a kind and loving decision Aaron' mother made. Some family, friends and loved ones may have been freaked out by the very idea of viewing Aaron and would not have wanted to remember him in a casket – seeing him in the casket would have been very painful and difficult, and that remembering him when he was alive was more than enough.

While some of Jeffers' family members may have found comfort in seeing Aaron as they remembered him, it may also have been uncomfortable and unbearable to others.

Eulogy Speech

When writing Jeffers' eulogy, Joy kept anecdotes in chronological order, to make it easier for her to organise her thoughts. Equally, it was easier for everyone in attendance to follow her speech.

Aaron's mother gave the eulogy. It was the ultimate honour for her to deliver her son's eulogy speech at his funeral.

"This was my way of praising him. It was very painful for me, particularly as his death was so unexpected and he was so young - in the prime of his life," Joy wrote.

It was an opportunity for Joy to share her love for her son, and to shed light on Aaron and what he was like as a person.

Joy wrote, "As I stepped up to the pulpit and stood in front of mourners and guests, the church was charged with emotion – it was natural to have an outpouring of grief.

It helped me to have my nephew, Simeon, join me on the podium for moral support during the reading of Aaron's eulogy. Just to have my nephew's presence beside me gave me the strength I needed to deliver my son's eulogy.

I did not cry at your funeral son, because I had no tears left. I have cried so much that I need to restock supplies."

It was very clear, Aaron was simply loved by all, and he made a huge difference in others' lives.

Other family members were mentioned in the eulogy - a few words on each family member's special relationship with Aaron was included.

The death of AJ was devastating to his mother, family members and friends.

There were lots of emotions all at once, with times when his family felt they were having a good day, and then they would wake up and feel worse again, overcome by an overwhelming sadness, anger and lots of tears. Powerful feelings came unexpectedly.

It was like waves on a beach where one minute they could be standing in water up to their knees and feel they could cope, then suddenly a big wave comes by and knocked them off their feet. Talking and sharing what his mother, family and friends felt with others helped to cope with the grief.

Joy will never ever get over the massive void, but in time will learn to live without Aaron's smile and voice. Trusting that Aaron is always by her side, helping her through troubled times, just as he used to do when he was here on earth and that his presence is around her always, constantly in her heart and always on her lips.

Aaron's mother had her wonderful son to love for 23 years and 6 months, and they both expressed how they felt about each other every single day. They both told each other *"I love you"* followed by Aaron's loving and affectionate warm hugs, which left the duo feeling safe, secure and loved. Aaron knew just how much Joy, his family and friends adored and loved him.

Joy read out loud:

"Good morning everyone. I introduce myself as Aaron's mother and I have here today Aaron's family and loved ones, including his son, who is a few weeks old. Today, we have the unenviable duties of celebrating Aaron's life and then saying farewell.

Let me first begin by thanking all of you here today out of love, respect and support for Aaron, for us as his parents and his family. Thank you for all of your cards, kind words and condolences. All of your presence, kindness and prayers have sustained us. We are humbled.

For those of you, who knew Aaron well, would know that he would jump in right now and lighten the moment for us on this day.

Proudly sporting his smart trendy attire and Converse trainers; with his beaming smile as bright as the sun; with his funny sense of humour, one liners or utter one of his astonishing Aaronisms. Then he would say, mom enough with the 'long ting.' Just tell a story or give a brief overview.

And Aaron would be right. Whether we are comfortable with it or not, we are left with the mysteriousness of life. The answers we are looking for are ultimately known only by the creator of all things, Jehovah God and his son Jesus Christ.

Aaron was and still is a wonderful man and a precious gift from Jehovah God to me, his family, and to all of us. Aaron will always be my special gift.

Here are a few short stories that celebrate who and what Aaron was, and is to me:

1. *Aaron always looked forward to waking up Christmas morning and spending time with me and his younger brother, talking about what presents we had brought each other. I used to pretend I had finished giving out the presents and would surprise both boys with more presents later. Aaron's vibrant smile was as big as the moon and he would always show his appreciation with his warm affectionate hugs and say 'I LOVE YOU mom, always.'*

2. *When Aaron was a teenager, I would take him to visit the late Grandad Jeffers on a Sunday. We would most certainly be greeted with food and drink, along with 'hands' of bananas which Grandad Jeffers and Aaron both loved.*

That particular Sunday, Grandad Jeffers had realised that Aaron had one of his ears pierced. Well in sheer disgust Grandad Jeffers took a huff and a puff and said "why on earth you go do something like that for and go tek needle bore up you ears hole like that. I don't know what is wrong with you young people" and continued moaning and mumbling under his breath. Aaron and I turned to each other and cried with so much laughter that Aaron replied, "I think Grandad is 'bex' you know mom, not 'vex'. Aaron was so fond of Grandad Jeffers and enjoyed spending quality time with him, for the simple reason he made Aaron laugh with this amusing stories and jokes. Aaron equally adored Grandad Lescott and Grandma France and always spoke very highly of them wherever he would go.

3. *Aaron was a conscientious team member of the ASDA workforce, attracting so many customers into the store with his stunning personality and exceptional customer service – also earning himself numerous awards for his efforts. Aaron did extraordinarily well in everything he put his mind to, and I am sure you would agree he was and is an asset to ASDA Perry Barr.*

4. *Aaron took pride in himself and has set a trend for his younger brother and many others. Looking good and feeling good was an important part of Aaron's daily life.*

5. *Beyond the Aaronisms, I have also tried to think about what Aaron would like us to walk away with today.*

• *Firstly, learn how to drive. It brought Aaron so much pleasure and happiness. I am sure we can find some in it too.*

• *Secondly, share what you know with others, in particular children and young people. Brighten their days. Give them the courage to push forward, to weather the storms and never ever give up, no matter what. Teach them to be responsible young men and women and make smart choices. Most of all, love and listen to them – they will make you smile when you least expect it.*

• *Thirdly, if you ever miss a loved one or someone else – write them a letter. Just get it all down on paper. Then you can rest for a bit. I encouraged Aaron to do the same when sharing my own personal experiences with him about life's challenges. I know that Aaron has himself written many letters as a way of expressing himself. He also encouraged others to write things down as a way of expressing themselves too, and they have all been the very best of friends ever since. Must have been good counsel Aaron gave.*

Some people think Aaron would have been a great father or uncle. Well, forget that – he was and still is a great father for so many children, including his sister and younger brother in so many ways – not forgetting his son, who Aaron has a deep love and passion for.

If you ever want to hang out with Aaron, you still can. Find a place where your memory takes you back to a special moment with Aaron that you remember. Aaron will be there, most likely cracking a smile, willing to listen to everything you have to say and leaving you feeling on top of the world with his sound advice. Like a genuine friend; like a caring brother; like a loving father; like a brave nephew and a fantastic son that Aaron is.

What more in these final moments can I say about my handsome son, Mr Aaron Silas Cephas Jeffers who has made me the proudest mother in the world for 23 years, 6 months and continues to bring me lots of joy with my beautiful grandson? What a wonderful mothers' day gift – the best ever.

These stories show us Aaron was immensely caring, tender-hearted, generous, a loving son a committed long-term partner to his girlfriend and a genuine and faithful friend to so many.

"I love you son, always and forever, mom" xx

It was during the reading of Aaron's eulogy to commemorate and celebrate his life by expressing and sharing thoughts, feelings and experiences out of honour and respect for him that Joy began to learn first-hand who her son really was.

Her emotions were all over the place - she felt shock, was overwhelmed and amazed that over 1,000 people from all cultures and walks of life turned up to say farewell and express how they loved her son, and discover how he inspired so many people, both young and old alike.

"I hope you realise Aaron what an impact you made on the world with your positive energy and vibration," expressed Joy.

There was not a dry eye in the church during the reading of the eulogy given by Jeffers' mother. Joy spoke of his life, his loves and how family and friends would continue to move forward in his absence.

There was so much sentiment and love - it is impossible to describe with words, and this comforted the family so much.

After the great tragedy and untimely passing, Joy now treasures five condolence books - a perfect way to share memories with Kwayme and her grandson; read written recordings of sympathy messages and cherish those farewell messages from all that knew him, including ASDA Perry Barr colleagues, customers, school teachers, friends and family.

Burial

Aaron is buried on the grounds of Witton Cemetery, Birmingham. The burial occurred later the same day around 12:30 pm. Aaron's mother, father, son, grandparents, siblings, cousins and close friends were all present.

Aaron's body was dressed in the colour red - his favourite colour, chosen by Joy and Kwayme: red snapback hat, red bomber jacket, red/blue tartan plaid checked button long sleeved shirt, dark raw denim straight leg Voi Jeans featuring detachable braces - Voi Jeans branding to front and rear and a pair of red and white Converse trainers. A family photo was placed in his hands, as a gift to preserve memories of family that they were very close to him.

Joy still considers her son to be a part of her family. He exists in memory and he continues to influence her family to this day. Whether Aaron's photo hangs on the wall has no bearing on his prominence in her family; but memories and moments involving him are an important part of his family's history.

The burial party was provided by family members, who were given the honour of carrying their relative across to the graveside and laying him to rest alongside his grandfather.

Music has the unique ability to speak to us when words fail, and that quality can comfort us at life's most difficult moments.

A selection of popular funeral hymns was sung during Aaron's burial to honour his memory – 'Abide With Me', 'The Old Rugged Cross' and 'In The Sweet By & By'.

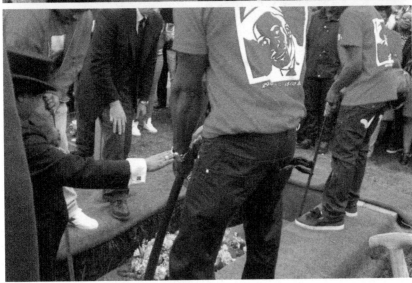

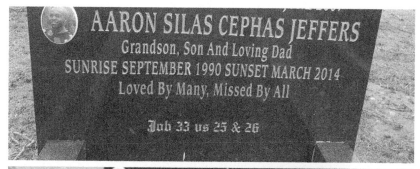

Floral Tributes

As a tribute to Aaron, ASDA Perry Barr arranged for beautiful fresh flowers to be delivered to the family home on the morning of his funeral, creating the perfect floral tribute to help loved ones express their love for AJ, at what was most certainly a difficult time for everyone who knew him.

The array of flowers on display - from wreaths to custom tributes in honour of Aaron's personality were placed on the drive of the family home before the funeral cars arrived to place them on top and beside Aaron's coffin. The flowers for Aaron's coffin were chosen by the immediate family.

There was also a selection of sympathy and condolence cards attached to the flowers, some of which were from ASDA Perry Barr, Birmingham friends and family with kind words written on them.

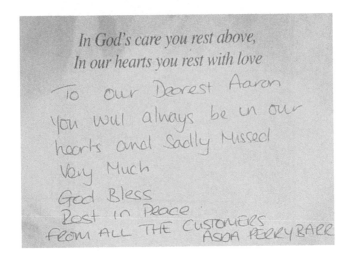

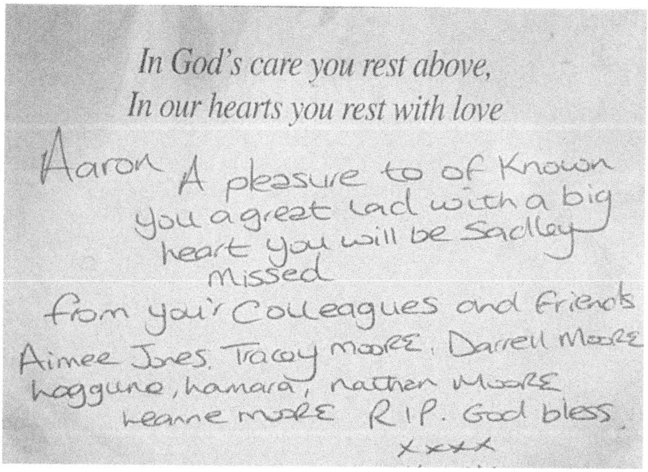

In God's care you rest above,
In our hearts you rest with love

Aaron A pleasure to of known
you a great lad with a big
heart you will be sadley
missed
from your Colleagues and friends
Aimee Jones, Tracey Moore, Darrell Moore
Laggune, hamara, nathen Moore
Leanne Moore RIP. God bless.
xxxx

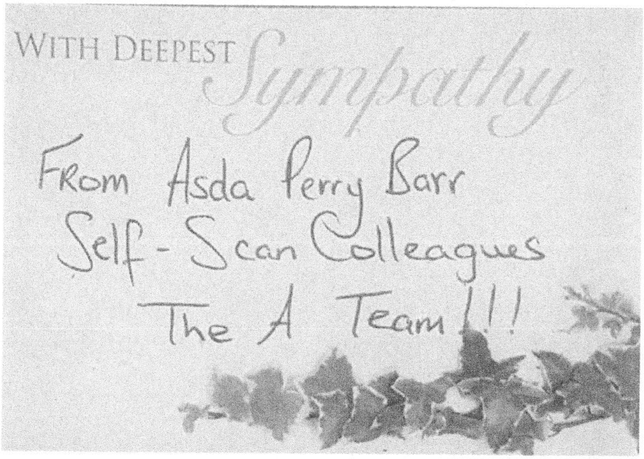

WITH DEEPEST *Sympathy*

From Asda Perry Barr
Self-Scan Colleagues
The A Team!!!

In Loving Memory

To our Colleague Aaron Jeffers
We are going to miss you so
very much, you will always be
in our hearts and thoughts
everyday
Goodnight and
sleep tight
God Bless
Rest in Peace
From All the Colleagues
Asda Perry Barr

Thinking of You

From Aaron's

friends and work
Colleagues.
Shantie, Sarah, Neka,
Linton, Audrey, Jas
and Sue

To Aaron
Love you
Dinesh & Jules
xxx
IN LOVING
MEMORY

In Loving Memory

R.i P
To A Wonderful
Cousin. Going to MISS
you SO MUCH!!
All my love.
from Debbie @
lauren, codie, Ethan
Dylan xx

In Loving Memory

To Aaron

Thank you for being a great friend. Im gonna miss you loads
R.I.P
Love Joel + family

In Loving Memory of Aaron Jeffers
your name stands out, you have
strenght & courage & you put up
a fight but God knows best
from Dave & family xx

With Deepest Sympathy

To Joy, Kwame + family.

I'm so sorry for your
loss of a wonderful
Person. Aaron was a truly
wonderful man + friend
I'll miss him so much . . . .

.... And his smile, you raised a
Perfect boy. Please stay strong
through this hard time
Love Joel + family

x x x x
R.I.P. Aaron Love you Bro

To AJ

Love you lots,

Catch you later
Sweetheart.
RIP xxxxx
IN LOVING
MEMORY.

To, FAMILY OF AARON JEFFERS.

SORRY FOR YOUR LOSS. AARON WAS AN
INSPIRATION TO ME AND OTHERS. ALWAYS
KEPT EVERYONE HAPPY & ALWAYS HAD A
SMILE ON HIS FACE. R·I·P TO A DEAR
FRIEND. HE WILL ALWAYS BE IN MY
HEART.
        LOVE GURJINDER CHOWLIA
                (MANSFIELD GREEN).

3756

A Sign Of Gratitude

Aaron's family thanked everyone who attended his funeral out of love, respect and support for him. They expressed their sincere thanks to all family members and friends for their cards, kind words, floral tributes and sympathy during their time of bereavement. Everyone's presence at Jeffers home coming, kindness and prayers sustained and humbled the family.

In speaking to so many people who attended Aaron's funeral, and in seeing the many postings that Aaron received on his Facebook page, his family learned even more than they already knew before how widely and deeply he was loved by all. Jeffers was so influential and impacted on the lives of many people.

"You had a very lovely colourful funeral service today son. I cannot believe I am saying that let alone telling you. I have never seen so much people in one space in my life. Everyone commented on how nice the service was. Giggles could be heard at the mention of some of your antics when I read out your eulogy and tributes were expressed from family and friends. We continued to celebrate your life in Ruskin Hall, Birmingham afterwards."

"My mind is blank now. I do not remember even leaving the house and getting into the funeral car. I just remember the slow journey to the church. I was very worried about Grandad Lescott because he told me before the church service that he was not strong enough to get through the day. I had to beg him to remain strong, as I needed his support to also get through a very difficult time in my life. He went missing after the church service and family members were looking for him, including myself. I discovered that Grandad Lescott had got on the coach, which he had arranged for people who wanted to attend your burial or who did not have transport of their own to get there. Grandad Lescott needed his own space. It was his way of trying to process what had just taken place – a deep loss for his grandson. He was not only mourning the loss of you, but he was also feeling my own pain of your suffering and me losing a child."

Mother's Eulogy Sentiments: 'My Hero'

"Aaron, I commend you for your amazing strength and bravery, particularly during the last 5 months of your wonderful life. I have always instilled in you from a very young age how important it is to never ever give up, no matter what you experienced in life. Giving up is the easy option, but having a positive mental attitude, with determination would bring you many achievements. You fought hard and you battled like a true soldier.

For that reason, you are my hero, my rock, my African warrior, my champion and my strength. You have made me a very proud mother. I love you always and forever." Mother xxxx

Kwayme's Eulogy Poem: 'My Brother Aaron'

"My brother Aaron everlastingly cared for me and my mother.

Aaron is funny, clever and is the best brother ever.

We even played on the Xbox happily together.

My loving brother taught me the importance of manners and respect, but most importantly, Aaron was just perfect.

My superb brother was a spectacular footballer.

He was the man of the show when scoring glorious goals for ASDA.

I will always remember and love my brother, Aaron always and forever."

Facebook Tributes

On 14th July 2017 at 04:13, Aaron's first cousin, Simeon wrote on his Facebook page:

"They say as the years go by it gets easier after losing a loved one, well I do not know about everyone else but with me, every year that goes by seems to get that much harder. Aaron Jeffers for me was not only my brother/cousin/best friend but he was also my go to guy whenever any problems arose. We had a mad/crazy connection like no other. When I had a problem, I would talk to him about it, then I would find out that he had been through it or was going through it. It was also the same whenever he had a problem, he would come and talk to me and he would discover that I had already gone through it or was going through it, so we

worked off each other throughout our lifetime. Now after 3 plus years he has passed, I am finding it hard to function and solve life's challenges without him being present.

Not a day, hour, minute or second passes that he does not pop up in my head from the smallest of things like laughing at cartoons I have seen thousands of times to seeing a smile on his son's face, or even playing play station/Xbox games and listening to music. It is just a constant reminder of what an impact he had on me and still having on so many people's lives. There is no one in this world like him.

He truly is one of his own kind and for being the person he was makes it so hard to move on in life without him by my side. I miss and love him so badly. There are not enough words to describe how I feel.

I now have his mother, my aunty/second mother as a positive/strong role model and devoted mother and grandmother as well as my own mother for strength and guidance – not forgetting the rest of our tight knitted family members in Birmingham/London that have helped along the way. Love you all xx

13ᵗʰ March 2020 Simeon writes: "6 years has flown by like no man's business, but losing you still feels ever so fresh in my heart. Not a day goes by that I don't think about you. Miss you so bad, it's unreal. Rest easy."

Family in London (Heather) responded to a comment Simeon had written on the same day on AJ's Facebook page:

"Yesterday the images of the T-shirts that the ushers wore at Aaron's home coming came to mind. Not knowing you were feeling so emotionally captivated by the emptiness in your heart. You have memories that no one has which will stay in your heart forever. There are some of us who although we are family DON'T have what you are blessed with. I don't have any cartoon memories. I know however you and your cousin remember just how long he would stay in the bathroom getting ready. We were going to Westfield White City a few months after it opened. We had to wait at least an hour if not longer for him to get ready. When we finally got there, we had to wait for him again as he explored Footlocker, JD Sports, Footasylum, Nike Store, Puma Store, Adidas and every other shop that sold trainers. HE WENT IN …. Finally, we selected a meeting place so WE could all go and do some shopping. Everything about him was IMMACULATE" xxxxx

13th March 2020 Heather writes "AJ you are one in a million."

Private Messages To Joy & Messages Featured On Aaron's Facebook Page

"I had the pleasure of meeting this incredible young man one day in ASDA. I looked at him and said, "I went to school with your father and your aunties." This youth was well spoken, polite and respectful. Sometimes you meet someone, and they touch the very core of your spirit, Aaron was such a person. From the bottom of my heart I send condolences to his family for raising this beautiful angel."

"RIP, beautiful smile, pure heart and always happy. Have left a print on my heart that I will never forget just by being you x."

"RIP, always smiling and always there to help x."

"Such a wonderful turn out for such a well-loved young man, RIP Aaron xx."

"I can only begin to imagine what a massive loss losing your beautiful son is. I hope you find some comfort in what his friends are posting on his Facebook page. He truly was amazing, and I always told him he was an angel. I look at his gorgeous face and remember how he had the knack of always saying the right things to make you feel better. You (mother) brought him up exceptionally well and I am sure you must be extremely proud. I hope his character and personality grow on in his son xx."

"My deepest sympathy to both you and your younger child. I can't believe to imagine how you as a mother must be feeling, to know your son has been taken so suddenly. A young fit and healthy man that had everything to live for, I am sure was so excited about the imminent birth of his first child."

Your younger son having to deal with the pain and the loss of his big brother at his tender age of 9, words fail me, but one must be strong, because as they say "life goes on" as you have witnessed first-hand with the birth of your grandson. Many congratulations as if by divine intervention a small token for mothers' day just to alleviate a little bit of the grief. Your grandson could never ever replace your beloved son Aaron, but to know you have something that is part of him may help over the coming weeks, months and years.

To lose a loved one isn't easy, but to lose a child must be the most painful of all. You will never get over the void but in time you will learn to live without

Aaron's smile, voice, but I am sure his presence will be around you always, constantly in your heart and always on your lips. The Lord works in mysterious ways. You had your wonderful son Aaron to love for 23 years. I remember the conversations you and I had, and you thought it was so important as a mother that you let your children know you love them, by telling them every single day. Keep your faith, turn to the Lord and he will comfort you. There's a lot of people praying and thinking about you during this sad time, me being one of them. Cry when you need to and remember it's not goodbye, it's until you meet. My love, big hugs and a kiss to you both- Kathleen Hicks xx".

"I cannot believe the news I woke up to this morning! We lost a great friend, dedicated colleague and all-around wonderful guy! Shifts at work haven't been the same and now they can't be again. I'm devastated and heartbroken :(RIP Aaron Jeffers. I miss our talks, the times we played football and most importantly you! You had a remarkable power for brightening up any day! I love you man! Heaven has a new angel now.

I still remember the shock of waking up to the news that morning. RIP Aaron Jeffers. You're still fondly remembered and deeply missed."

"It's so strange I was just looking at Aaron's picture on the self-scan and was thinking it's been a while since he's gone, but still so fresh in our memory without realising today is the day (13th March 2020).

"6 years already WOW. RIEP Jeffers. My heart will always be broken. Truly and honestly, I'm glad I met you. You touched many lives xxx (13th March 2020).

RIP Aaron. I never got to meet you :(Rest easy in the arms of the angels xx (13th March 2020).

"Always in my heart" xxx (13th March 2020)

"Forever in my heart" xx (13th March 2020)

YouTube Tributes

RIP Aaron - The Funeral Was Today

"So I have been sitting here for about 1 ½ hours listening to Eminem, trying to get my head around this. A very good friend of mine, someone who I highly respected passed away today. He suffered from a heart attack a while back and he was in a coma from what I believe to be what happened. I got the text message off a friend who when I read it, it was like a body shock. I was just stuck to the

ground. I was just … I just cannot believe that this would happen to someone like this person. His name is Aaron Jeffers. I met him when I worked at ASDA Perry Barr, Birmingham or Walmart for those watching in America, but we call it ASDA here. For the years that I was there and Aaron was there with me, we both ran that place – we felt like we did. From the moment I met Aaron, I had the upmost respect for him because he just approached me and shook my hand and said "Hello." That to me is a great sign of respect to just walk up to a total stranger, shake their hand and say hello and introduce themselves. From that day, we just … we just … There is no words, no words. I cannot even describe what I am feeling right now. It's just … so taken back by this and I tried to plan this video. I tried to record it with emotion and I was getting too upset. I was trying to record it in a happy way because I felt that Aaron would not want me to be unhappy and I just could not get through it. The only thing I could do is approach this from the heart right now. That is probably why I sound so jaded. This is hard. This is probably the hardest video I have ever had to make. Let me just tell you that Aaron – you could just tell he was raised perfectly. He had such positive influences around him. Aaron had wonderful parents. He was just born with standards and morals and respect for other people. I had a similar family and this is why I was drawn to him. Aaron was just a perfect person. That is the only way I can explain who he was. He was a perfect individual, who was always up for doing stuff. He was healthy, fit and always playing football, doing sports. He was always happy and positive. He was always diplomatic and fair. Aaron never got involved in drama. He was the sort of person you could share your whole life problems to and he would sit there and listen. He was a very very intelligent soul, and would provide his peers with sound advice and help you out with whatever you needed - he was willing to because he was just that sort of person. Aaron was just a perfect person and it is really really heart-breaking that someone of his calibre, someone as special and as important as he is would be taken away. Now, I am not a religious person at all, but I know that he was and his family are. If there is a heaven, if there is such things Aaron is going to be running that place in a week, trust me. Aaron was a phenomenal person and I am going to miss him, I really am. There are a lot of times when I would talk to him when I was coming into ASDA, or just to shop and I would seek out to talk to him because he was the sort of person I would reach out to talk to. There are not a lot of people in my life that have been like that. We always talked about work and jobs because I had left ASDA and I was moving on. Aaron's positivity and his attitude just made me change who I am. He changed my life. Aaron is the reason why I am doing teaching at the moment because I was speaking to him one time and said "Aaron, I don't know whether to carry on into security or try and get into teaching." He looked at me and said "Well what do you want to do with your life." I said "I have always wanted to be a Teacher." Aaron looked at me and said "Well, go and do it." I did and I am training to become a Teacher now. Aaron has really impacted my life and my personality and meeting him was a true true honour, to know him and have him as a genuine friend. It was not like we were best friends seeing each other outside work, it was just like a work-friendship and just mutual respect. I cannot imagine how his family, girlfriend and people who saw him every day feel because if Aaron's passing has affected me like this, it must be the greatest loss to them possible. My condolences go out to Aaron's family who knew him and loved him like I did. I hope that you can take solace in the fact that Aaron was a true, genuine, honest and respectful person. He was one of a kind – a special type of guy. I'm sure it was not just me that he impacted while he was here. If there is such a thing as fate or things that are meant to happen, then I can only take Aaron's attitude and his positive energy into my life and live what I can to the fullest in memory of him – in honour of him. So Aaron, if you are watching or listening, I love you man, I really do. I am really going to miss you and I hope wherever you are that you are at peace and that you are happy. Peace out – take care." - Barry Hart.

Facebook response from Marvin Dean Palmer to Barry Hart on 13th March 2014 featured on Aaron's Facebook page:

I'm proud of what you have done and I'm sure when Aaron's family watch your video, your memories they too will have memories of him. They will be heartfelt and proud. Everything you have mentioned is to a "T". Everything what Aaron stands for is a reflection of his mother – well mannered, happy, joyful, courageous, proud, committed and striving for the best. Aaron will be missed on a massive scale. I have seen Aaron rise from being a boy to a man, and he has made me proud, regardless how he was short lived. He had made me proud from his accomplishments and his way of living. Aaron will be missed for sure. Another bright face taken away from us, but will never be forgotten. His spirit will forever shine and protect us. RIP Aaron "Bow Wow" Jeffers." - Marvin Dean Palmer.

This video is about a funeral I attended today. If you remember about a week ago, I realised a video called RIP Aaron, which is about my good friend Aaron Jeffers who sadly passed away. Today was his funeral 13th March 2014. It was a crazy day; it was like an emotional rollercoaster. Firstly, I attended the church service. It was a really beautiful looking church, and inside was really big, really modern. I have not been in many churches, but I was thoroughly impressed with the church and the ceremony as a whole. I actually have the order of service which I am going to keep forever (order of service shown to viewers). I will show you some pictures of Aaron. There is one thing you can see from all of these pictures that Aaron has the Jeffers smile as I would like to call it. It was a smile that was so big; it would infect anyone else to smile as well. That was one of the greatest things about Aaron. It was just a crazy day. I have never been on such an emotional rollercoaster in my life. There were obviously tributes and hymns and bible readings and such things. The tributes were really good. It was just genuine people speaking with genuine feelings and not just this normal cliché stuff that you hear at funerals. It was awesome and everyone who read the tributes and sung songs they really held it together. They were really strong. I was really impressed that they could get through what they had to say because I don't think that if it was me I would not have been able to get through it. There were some really touching moments and my lips were quivering and my eyes were watering. I was tearing up and everything. That was to be expected because Aaron was such an amazing guy. It got to the eulogy, read by Joy Lescott, his mother. I was expecting tears and upset, but Joy was really really impressive to me – such a strong woman and just got through everything she needed to say with conviction. If it was one of my children, if I had children it would be an impossibility to get through those things that she had to get through. There were lots of stories and memories and anecdotes about Aaron – little things that you kind of forget like his vaseline that he carried on him, which his mother mentioned in the eulogy. When that was mentioned in the eulogy, that had me in bits because all I can remember now is every day working with Aaron he would have this small tub of vaseline in his trouser pocket and he would be rubbing it on his hands to keep them moist throughout his ASDA shifts. It was such a good moment. There were lots of good moments. The thing for me from his father Stephen Jeffers was that he was so upbeat and positive. He got everyone out of their sadness and pulled everyone together as one big family and we all celebrated Aaron's life instead of mourning his death. I think that is what Aaron would have wanted and it is definitely what his family wanted. It was a perfect send off for such a great person like Aaron. The thing that got me through, and I just don't know how I did not cry more was the song that his father dedicated to Aaron at the church – Dance With My Father (Luther Vandross). It was a song that Aaron had chosen for his father's funeral, but obviously Aaron passed away and that song was a tribute from his father to his son. I was just completely gone, my eyes were just streaming – face wet. It was an incredible turn-out. I have seen weddings which have less people turn up for. From what I could estimate, I did not really count everyone in the church – I would say there were about 800 people present in the church, possibly close to 1,000. Those numbers did not thin out. When I went to the graveside, there was about 400 – 500 people there around one little grave. It was incredible. I have never seen anything like it. It was a really touching moment around the graveside – to have all of Aaron's brothers, family and friends shovelling the dirt. It was amazing how strong everyone was and I want to commend everyone in Aaron's family who was just so strong today because it was how Aaron was, and it is how he was raised. I could see Aaron throughout his entire family. It was what I needed. I needed this to happen to be able to accept what has happened. From the moment I had found out that Aaron had passed away, I have struggled with it – really struggled with it. I made the RIP Aaron video on the day that I found out and I was really upset. Since then, I am not going to lie I have felt sorry for myself. I have felt guilty. I have been angry. I suppose they are just the stages of grief, but now I know that I need to be Aaron. I need to be happy. I need to be positive and do things in life that are right for me and do them to the fullest of my ability and look out for people and help people and to have all this stuff that I have had in me for my entire life that I may have forgotten about. These things have been instilled in me by Aaron's family. Thank you Joy and Stephen for such a great send off. The chats that I had with you personally Joy really meant a lot to me and I am really happy that I got to meet you Joy face to face because we have obviously only spoken to each other over Facebook beforehand. It was really strange to have people coming up to me and saying "Are you the guy that made the RIP Aaron video?" All of the other people that I met were phenomenal. I felt a bit embarrassed because I was not used to people caring about what I had to say because it was not like I had said anything different to what someone else would have said about Aaron. It was so surreal and that is why it has been an emotional rollercoaster. Thank all of the Lescott and Jeffers family for all that you have done today because it was perfect. Aaron would have been proud. I was proud and I am sure all of you were proud as well. Towards the end of the day I was trying to escape from the after party because I knew what was about to happen. I went to say my goodbyes and Stephen wanted me to make a speech in front of everyone. I said "I cannot do this – I just cannot do it." Out of respect for Stephen asking me and in memory of Aaron, I was honoured to be asked to do it. It was the hardest thing I had ever done. I cannot even remember what I said in the actual speech. It was like a blur and a haze. I hope that it was all good. I hope I did well. Thank you Stephen for asking me to be the first person to speak and I was honoured that you would look to me to make a speech about your son, who was a great person and will live on in everyone, especially me. I will take on all of Aaron's attributes I can from his personality and I am going to put them in my life and I am going to go as far as I can in the memory of him. I will never forget Aaron and I am sure his family will not either. Thank you for having such a great son, who influenced and changed my life. Mr Jeffers may you be at rest my friend." – Barry Hart.

Book Of Condolences

When the first reports came in of the death of Aaron, most of those who knew him were sleeping, unaware of the tragedy. By the time people heard the news, a lot of the rest of the world already knew and had started trying to explain exactly what AJ had meant to them.

The local community soon joined in paying their tributes and did so with a fervour and intensity which took many people back. Ordinary people - the kind of people Aaron had met in the ASDA Perry Barr, Birmingham supermarket -- saw their tributes join those of family, friends and people from all walks of life.

The public show of emotion continued unabated, however, and queues started forming at ASDA Perry Barr, Birmingham to sign books of condolence. The more people queued and the more books that were made available, the more people seemed to want to take part.

It is hard to believe so much time has passed since AJ's tragic death that led to such an outpouring of grief locally and regionally.

The books of condolence were opened a day after the death of Aaron on 13th March 2014. It allowed visitors to the ASDA Perry Barr, Birmingham Superstore to express their thoughts and find comfort.

ASDA Perry Barr was thronged with people after the announcement of Aaron's death, of every degree and condition, race and religion, seeking a place of comfort in their grief, to say a prayer, to leave a posy of flowers, to express their sadness in their own words by writing a message in his family's Books of Condolence.

Jeffers' death resulted in an outpouring of public grief and sympathy. To help bring light to the whole bereaved ASDA Community, including parents and family's hearts, hundreds and thousands of ASDA customers offered their kind and heartfelt words of comfort to Aaron's family for their loss. They offered personal messages of support and understanding as a way of acknowledging that they too were grieving. They wanted to show they cared about Aaron and his family as part of the grieving process.

The family appreciate that writing condolence messages for Aaron, must have been a difficult task because of the deep emotion that was involved in the writing.

With over a 1,000 people, some of which travelled to Birmingham to watch the funeral cortege, it was clear that the simple act of attendance was the chosen act of remembrance.

In fact, at least 5 books of condolence were filled, covering several hundred pages to stand for so many of the sentiments people who had the pleasure of knowing Jeffers felt bound to commit to paper:

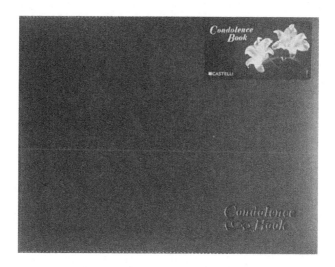

"To Joy, words are not enough to express how sorry I am that you have lost your beautiful son. I never met him but from the love and passion which you spoke about him, I know he was a mature, loving young man. I know he would be extremely proud of you and for the way you took care of him and kept your family together. I'm sure his child will express all those wonderful qualities and morals he cherished. May you find comfort in his memories, the hugs and smiles you shared. He is safe in Jehovah's loving memory. Isaiah 40:29-31."

"To you and family, words absolutely fail me at the moment for the loss of your son and the birth of your grandson. Love and regards."

"To the mother of a very special person. May God bless, guide and protect you and also be blessed as Aaron's mother. Peace and blessings."

"Congratulations on becoming a grandmother. Your grandson will bring you so much happiness. Aaron lives on through his son. Love and best wishes."

"To all the family, thinking of you all at this sad time. We were the paramedics who attended to Aaron and also a friend of your son who knew him for a long time. Aaron will be deeply missed. God Bless."

"To my friend, you were there when I needed a friend – I've never forgotten! Just a small token of my love. Spoil yourself. Aaron would've wanted that. All my love."

"Condolences to the family of Mr Aaron Jeffers. He was such a pleasant and approachable soul. Always ready to help. May God bless and keep him close within the spiritual realm."

"RIP Aaron. You were the JOY of ASDA Perry Barr, Birmingham with your jokes and lovely smile."

"Such a well-mannered young man, RIP Aaron. You will be missed but always in our hearts."

"Aaron, you will be sadly missed. Shopping here will never be the same as I was always greeted with your lovely smile. RIP lovely."

"Sorry to hear the passing of Aaron. You should be proud to have such a wonderful, helpful and handsome son. God Bless."

"Very sorry to hear this incredibly sad news. I remember Aaron as a very pleasant and polite young man. I even commended him to ASDA Management. So sad. Deepest sympathy to family and friends."

"To Aaron's family and friends, deepest condolences on your loss. We had the pleasure of knowing him as one the nicest, genuine person you could ever wish to know, always smiling (genuinely)."

To Aaron, my beloved son. I miss you so very much and love you endlessly. You have made me the proudest mother in the world. You will live on in my memory forever and ever amen - mom."

"Aaron, your death has been a real shock to all of us. We are praying for the family."

"*To Joy, it's so inspiring and encouraging to see Aaron doing so much better in the hospital. His strength is remarkable, and I don't need to tell you he has a worlds worth of people behind him, praying for him. It brought joy to my heart to see some of the reactions he gave to me when I was talking to him. I continue to have faith and believe in the strength Aaron has shown as I have seen first-hand Aaron's single most strengthening aspect – his family. The strength and belief exhibited by yourself and your family has been eye-opening, and I know Aaron is as proud of you as you are of him. I'm glad that Aaron has such amazing people in his life, and it brings me hope. Take care and stay strong, with love.*"

"*RIP Aaron, you were a wonderful and blessed young man, whom any mother would be proud to call their son. Your smile will be missed. Rest in the arms of the Lord my son.*"

"*RIP Aaron, never a day went by you didn't smile, never a dull shopping trip with you around. God bless.*"

"*RIP you brighten up this world. Your smile, your wonderful persona. You will be missed an angel on earth. My condolences to your family and friends. ASDA has lost a top employee – willing and hardworking, RIP.*"

"*Absolutely no words!! Sad loss – not only for the ASDA family but for the local community. Always remember your smiling face.*"

"*Aaron, you will be sadly missed. Only knew you for a short while, but you made such an impact. Watch from above and see how much of an impact you have made on this world.*"

"*RIP Aaron Jeffers. We will always remember you. You will be sadly missed bro as we did a lot together. You have touched the heart of many, including me. Love from your big brother, who is over 40 (a joke you used to share with me in ASDA).*"

"*Just came into ASDA and read messages. Looks like I missed out meeting a great young man. RIP Aaron.*"

"*Oh my God!! Aaron. I just found out that you are no longer here with us. You are one, no the best worker, friend which I have developed from coming into this ASDA. My wife and I truly do miss you Aaron. May your spirit be at a loving and peaceful place. Thank you, Aaron RIP. God bless.*"

"*Aaron, pupil, son, friend – Aaron attended Mansfield Green Primary School from the age of 4 to 11 years. He was an excellent pupil who was a pleasure to teach. The staff remembers Aaron for his smile, calm manner, sense of humour and charm, along with his willingness of learn. He was a ray of sunshine to the class and always had positive things to say about his peers. Aaron had a love for football from an early age and was in the School Football Team. He did extremely well and was an outstanding team player. When he left to go to secondary school, he would always return and ask how we were doing. Whenever a member of staff from Mansfield School went into ASDA, he would also greet them with a big smile and ask how they were doing. On the news of his death, school went into mourning. Aaron will be greatly missed by all. We pray that God will strengthen and comfort his family."*

"As a mother I cannot imagine your pain but as I always say, Aaron was most definitely an earth angel wise beyond his years and always saying the right thing or just his smile. WOW what a smile. I think about him often and about you, his son, his loved ones. May you continue to find comfort in each other and when you are really low just remember one he is around and two he was such a special young man who must be spreading his joy elsewhere now.

"Aaron is very special to a lot of people. I met him in ASDA Perry Barr, Birmingham as I'm sure so many people did. I was in there a lot as I work in the community with learning disabilities. We became friends and we would just chat about general stuff. I was having a really difficult time with something at work, extremely difficult and he picked up on it without me saying a word. He would communicate with me just at the right time – when I needed some comfort without prior knowledge. I will always remember him as he touched my heart and my soul. I have a son who I am extremely proud of and love with all my heart, but your son wasn't one in a million. He was on a completely different level. I'm not religious at all, but I am spiritual and Aaron was definitely an angel.

I cannot imagine your pain. You too are a remarkably strong lady to have been blessed with such a beautiful son. I hope you find comfort in Aaron's son, your beautiful grandson.

I have no doubt your grandson is gorgeous inside and out. These are not qualities that can be taught alone as you say beautiful souls and we have no bearing on our soul – it is a gift. I miss you my perfect earth angel always and forever. Love to you all and lots of love RIP.

I think of you often Aaron as you pop up first on my friend list and in my phone contacts. I miss your kind words of wisdom beyond your years. You never failed to make me smile and feel instantly better." – Sharon Butler xxx

"I met Aaron around 1997 when he was 7 years old, as I lived next door to his brother, Jerome Jeffers. I was not aware at that time that they were both brothers. As a child, I remember Aaron and Jerome knocking on my nan's door

asking me to play outside. Even when my nan said "no" I could not play out, Jerome and Aaron would still knock on my nan's door at every opportunity, regardless. Nan would respond every single time "no girl pickney in a dis house is playing out a door."

Some years later, I met Aaron while shopping in ASDA. He served me with his classic bright smile and greeted me with manners. As time went by, shopping in ASDA became a pleasure all due to Aaron. Despite the length of the queues and the amount of items, when Aaron was serving customers on the tills he insisted that he served me.

One day he asked me for my number, and I replied "We only do BBM (Black Berry Messenger) around here bab." We would both hold many BBM conversations and have numerous jokes and banter in ASDA.

Throughout my shopping experiences at ASDA, Aaron would just pop up out of no-where in the ASDA isles and somehow would manage to add extra shopping – random items to my trolley and then insist that he was serving me at the till he was operating from at the time of his shift. It would take me twice the time to load my shopping onto the conveyor belt separating my shopping from Aaron's mischievous shop that was not needed. I now see why Aaron done this. It was his way of spending twice the time with me to hold jokes and banter, but then why wouldn't he?

If anyone was to ask me what was Aaron's highlight for his ASDA shifts, it would be the number of fans (or as I would call it, his fans – school ties) that would come to see him at the end of their day.

I became aware of Aaron and Jerome being brothers on BBM, as one or the other posted a birthday picture and message on their phone, celebrating one's birthday. This shocked me. I then had a light bulb moment. It suddenly hit me. I realised at that moment, Aaron was the other young boy that would knock on my nan's door back in 1997 asking me to play out.

Beyond all the jokes and banter, Aaron had a sensitive, kind and caring heart. He showed this to me back in 2011 when I had just discovered one of my relatives had become terminally ill. I had gone to ASDA to purchase some items, along with a balloon for my Uncle. Aaron was on his lunch break at the time, so I approached the Customer Service Desk to request some helium for the balloon. I was informed by the Customer Service staff that ASDA did not have any helium in store at the time. Out of nowhere, Aaron appeared and could sense something was wrong with me because I was not my normal bubbly self. Even though he was on his break, he hugged me and took the time to find out what was wrong.

Eventually, I opened up to Aaron and explained. Aaron demonstrated his support with his kind words and told me that he was there for me whenever I needed to talk or off-load. Aaron took my balloon and asked me to stay put. He explained that he would be back soon. 5 minutes later, Aaron returned with an inflated balloon bouncing alongside him. Aaron handed me the balloon and embraced me with a hug and a promise to 'shout me' a bit later. From knowing the type of guy Aaron was, I'm sure he kept to his word.

Since Aaron has passed away, ASDA has not been the same. However, I have had the opportunity to get to know and build a relationship with his mom, Joy. We are able to share all of our memories together about Aaron. Joy is Aaron's mom, but to me, she is a friend that's always there. Aaron, if you were not a part of my life, your mom wouldn't be able to be a part of my life now. So for that, thank you bab.

Aaron, you have left us here on earth in person, but you are here with us in spirit of every day, of every moment. I will cherish every moment you were a part of my life, and I will do my best to honour them with a smile, but I guess not as big as yours. Love and miss you loads down here. Rest In Peace." – Sarah Francis xx

"Aaron, you were such a good soul, unrepeatable. RIP."

"Nothing was ever too much. No matter the time of day, you always had a kind word to say and a smile on your face. Thank you, Aaron. You'll be sorely missed."

"To an amazing gentleman. You always made me smile and had a positive energy that you promoted. May you rest in peace."

"It's very sad to see one very helpful, peaceful and admirable young person to leave us. RIP. You will be missed dearly."

"Aaron always wore an adorable smile on his face. It was enough to cheer me up when I was feeling blue. I did not know Aaron, except the odd few occasional smiles and hellos, but I knew that he was a sweetheart. RIP."

"Sorry to hear such a great young man has left us so early on in his/our life, but the time you spent here with us was wonderful. I only knew you to say hello and thank you to on my weekly shop, but boy didn't I look out for you – a person I called friend and Shop Assistant. RIP Aaron."

"Hey Aaron, so sorry I couldn't make it to see you off yesterday. I heard your mum has been keeping strong. She is such an inspiration. Congratulations on the birth of your beautiful son. I know you would have made a brilliant dad. You were

truly a lovely person, such a loss to see you have gone so soon. Keep on smiling."

"All the customers will miss your jolly personality, warm smile and cheerful disposition. You will certainly be missed. RIP."

"To the family of Aaron Jeffers, it's hard to bury our children, loved ones. May Jehovah God bless and guide you during your time of sorrow Psalms 23."

"RIP Aaron, you had an infectious smile and beautiful personality. God Bless baba."

"You were a very lovely, kind and always cheerful young man to all, always smiling no matter the time of day. That's all being a human to others means. You lived to this expectation and your example of the love of God to all will live on here in ASDA. We love you so much, but he loves you most. He said "come home my faithful servant. Have a rest. Job well done."

"I didn't know you very well, but when I saw you in ASDA, I felt you were my son. May God comfort your family, and may you rest in peace."

"RIP Aaron, always smiling, always happy, always friendly and more than willing to help. A good kid, kind hearted. May God take care of your soul."

"I was helped out by this young man at ASDA Perry Barr on many an occasion. Helpful, professional and too much potential for such a loss. As someone that knew him briefly in passing, he made his mark. God Bless the family at this time – ASDA Customer and conversationalist with Aaron Jeffers."

"To Aaron's family, I am sorry to hear about Aaron's passing. You raised a very pleasant and friendly young man who was a pleasure to be around. I was privileged to have met him. God Bless."

"Aaron, I miss your face on the self-service check out, guiding us along. RIP, gone too soon."

"Aaron, you always had a smile at work. You were an excellent representation of ASDA. Always very helpful."

"I am sorry to hear of your loss. You were an absolute credit to everyone around you. You brightened up everyone's day with your infectious, loving and caring nature. You will be sadly missed, and I pray that your family and soon to be are tremendously blessed."

"To my dear friend, what a great loss – we are speechless. One of your favourite words "one of the greatest men!" You will be greatly missed."

"To Aaron's family, your son was a credit to you. Sorry for your loss."

"Aaron, what a wonderful sweet boy you are, your spirit will remain the same. We had many a laugh in ASDA. RIP."

Dealing With Grief After The Funeral

The funeral happened and the intensity of activity stopped overnight. Calls from concerned friends and family were less frequent; cooked meals stopped arriving and friends and family were getting on with their lives. The flowers from the funeral began wilting.

Joy's memory of Aaron began to absorb her thoughts and she started to wonder how her son became so ill. Was it caused by stress? Why did Aaron not tell her he was sick sooner – Aaron often explained to his mother, *"I'm a big man now and can look after myself, you don't need to worry about me."* How long was Aaron suffering in silence before the medics got involved?

But in the period after the funeral, the real work of dealing with grief and mourning began for Joy and her family. It was vital for her to give herself space and time to get in touch with what was going on. Eventually, she began putting a gentle routine into place, eating well and took regular walks to build a good foundation for dealing with the difficulty of her son's loss.

Joy continues her connection with Aaron by visiting him at his grave. She still wants to love Aaron in his absence, as the feelings she has for him has not died or altered in any way, and never will. Their relationship had just transformed.

Joy wrote: *"Son, a spiritual thing keeps happening to me when I am out driving. I see your initials in car licence plates. For example "AJ64"; "AZJ"; "AYJ" and "AEJ". Each time I experience this, it brings a big smile to my face. Is this your way of letting me know you are okay, or that you are watching over me?*

I could be alone, with friends or family when you suddenly pop to mind with your 'Spiritual SMS' messages. We all look at each other trying to process what just happened. We all did it, but it was not until I pointed it out to others that I was not just seeing things, that they also realised.

There are many intuitive people who receive signs and messages while driving – communicating with spiritual guides through car licence plates. I know because I am one of them. After researching spiritual numbers and what 'Spiritual Number 64' means, it all finally makes sense. Your message is asking me to figure out what it is that I really want to do with my life. What is it that truly makes me happy, feel alive, and inspired. I see your message clearly whilst driving trying to urge me to investigate myself and start doing what I am supposed to be doing – to be my authentic self. Spiritual Number 64 is a message from you to encourage me to stay grounded and focused, knowing that I am always supported, as I work on my Divine life purpose and path. This number indicates that the hard work and effort one puts into their endeavours will have long-term benefits for them and their loved ones, and they are encouraged to keep up the great work.

'AJ9 Forever', a community group was set up for you my darling by your secondary school mates, as a way for everyone who knew you to show all their love and appreciation for you as a friend and brother. Spiritual Number 9 is a symbol that you are truly blessed. This number symbolises love, faith, spiritual enlightenment. Jehovah God gave us the gift of life; it is up to us to give ourselves the gift of living well.

"Today, Sunday 21st June 2020 – Father's Day, I visited you at your resting place. Accompanied with me was a dear friend of yours, Sarah Francis. She is a dear friend to me too. We came to see you today as a way of honouring your fatherhood and paternal bond to your son, as well as clearing up your headstone and surrounding resting quarters. We all know how important cleanliness was to you.

As you can imagine, it was understandably busy here today at Witton Cemetery, Birmingham. It was so peaceful. There were lots of people visiting their loved ones just like me and Sarah was - leaving flowers on their father's or son's graves and paying their respects. As Sarah and I were clearing up, a car had driven by. I looked up and I noticed the car registration number plate 'AJ59.' I had a moment of sudden enlightenment and realised that you were sending me another spiritual message. I grabbed my phone before leaving the cemetery and researched the meaning of Spiritual Number 57 to be able to decode the message that you were trying to convey.

The number 5 has a vibration of major life changes, learning, adaptability, idealism, good life choices, intelligence and versatility. The number 7 signifies spiritual awakening and spiritual enlightenment, peace, faith, mysticism, empathetic abilities, wit, introspection, spirituality, adventure, inspiration, inner wisdom and intuition. The number 7 also implies creative expression. Number 57 people are capable of creating art works or have an unusually creative way of communicating. These people love writing and can be very good at creative writing.

They enjoy expressing themselves in writing, where they can express their personal freedom and their inner self. Number 57 people, although creative themselves, often support other people's creativity and raise their optimism.

Thank you so much for your uplifting message today son. Your message had a special meaning just for me at that particular moment. Seeing you today on Father's Day was confirmation to encourage me to rely on my intuition and inner wisdom to guide me during this important life change and transformation that I am currently experiencing, following the path of my Divine life purpose and soul mission – which is writing.

Grandson, I write from my heart, from a place of love and caring for you. I hope:

- *I have helped provide a way for you to connect generations through your father by sharing my story about his life with you from memories that have bubbled to the surface.*

- *This book helps your mind work through events and emotions; reveals your father's history and what shaped his life; leaves you with a recorded history to help you better understand your own history; brings light to just how powerful, loving and beautiful your father really was.*

- *This important gift – a gift that will literally last forever provides you with a unique first-hand account of your culture and personal history that others do not have.*

I hope I have done you proud." xx

Sometimes out of nowhere single white feathers float down by me, or I will find them in unusual places. There are no birds in sight when this happens. It just appears out of thin air. This is so unreal that I had to do some digging into what it could mean. Here is what I found. Finding a white feather can mean a guardian angel is watching over you. It can also mean feathers are signs from a loved one who has passed on. Events like these just cannot be random, they must have meaning. The feathers definitely put a smile on my face and made me feel extremely comfortable."

I have noticed the presence of red robins flying into the garden since that time. I was having some work done in the garden. The red robin flew close to me and started walking around the area where the work was taking place. The red robin would not budge. The workman told me that each time I went indoors to make cups of tea, the red robin would fly away. As soon as I returned, the red robin would fly back and re-appear. This reminded me of when you were in the hospital and I came to see you at your bedside. During my visits, the doctors would want 5 minutes of my time to meet with me in private to provide updates on your situation. You would become a little uneasy. I sensed you thought in your mind that I came to visit you and not the doctors and that we both needed each other's attention, rather than the focus being on the doctors. Again, I decided to research what sighting of red robins meant. I was curious. To my surprise, the red robin is a sacred bird that offers protection and spiritual enlightenment. If a red robin keeps visiting you, it indicates you have encountered a loss of someone you love and that they are watching over you. The red robin is encouraging you to be brave again. When I saw the red robin, it made my day and brought me a lot of comfort, connecting with you and the beautiful nature. Thank you for your visit Mr 'AJ' Robin. I am very much looking forward to hanging out with you again soon during the springtime season."

Aaron was a natural lightworker and had an innate sense of wisdom about life for such a young man. He was a charitable individual. His life purpose had much to do with service to other people around him, as his positive vibes touched people's lives and those of his loved ones. He provided a source of strength, moral support, enlightenment, motivation, kindness and laughter in peoples' lives, which lead them towards the path of success. His ability to empathise with others was his best trait, one that was used to the fullest to provide solace to other people, especially his loved ones. His compassionate heart was the true source of comfort he offered to those around him, as proof that he could be relied upon. It is very clear to see, Aaron had no qualms offering his life to serving other people both within the ASDA community, and to society.

Remember, it does not matter how we express our grief, if we find a way that resonates with us. It might be that you decide to use your creative skills to remember your loved one. This could consist of writing a book; creating collages and memory boxes; playing music; writing poetry or connecting with nature. We need to recognise our feelings, give them a name and then find a way to express them.

"Keep your head up. Jehovah God gives his hardest battles to his strongest soldiers."

"Going into ASDA after your death was very challenging for me. I expected you to sneak up behind me like you used to, blind fold my eyes with your warm hands. How you always knew I was in ASDA shopping to this day I will never know. You would always say 'What we having for dinner today mom?' with that deep manly voice of yours."

"ASDA was not the same without you after you passed – staff left to take up new opportunities, whilst others probably moved on as they felt your loss was too much for them to handle. How did food shopping and browsing get so hard?" expressed Joy.

AJ was very aware his mother felt very ill during the time of his sickness and sacrificed his own situation out of concern for her. He pleaded with other family members to look after his mamma, ensuring she was okay. Her hair was breaking; her body was riddled with so much pain and she was rapidly losing weight. Joy found herself getting a health MOT at her GP Practice and follow-up consultations after her loss.

When Joy arrived at the surgery and saw her GP, she explained she had just laid her son to rest and opened up about health symptoms she had been experiencing. The GP responded, *"Did your son work at the ASDA Perry Barr Store, Birmingham and was his name Aaron?"*

Joy confirmed, *"Yes."*

Was my GP psychic? The GP added, *"I know Aaron very well. He served both me and my husband many times in ASDA. What a polite, helpful and well-mannered individual he was, and you should be very proud of him."*

The GP's kind words somehow comforted Joy through her grief and pain. The GP re-assured Joy she would get better over time, and she did.

"I found myself going back to the times when Aaron used to attend the surgery with me as a child and as a patient, which was very rare. My mind kept flashing back to when Aaron visited the surgery initially when he took ill (confirmed by Aaron's medical records). I wonder what must have been on his mind, I also wonder how he must have been feeling at the time?" Joy wrote.

Grief becomes a part of how we love a person despite their physical absence; it helps connect us to memories of the past; it bonds us with others through our shared humanity, and it helps provide perspective on our immense capacity for finding strength and wisdom in the most difficult of times.

Remembrance Anniversaries

Taking the time to honour and remember a loved one's death anniversary is about reconnecting and re-affirming our on-going relationship with the deceased.

It was essential to Joy's mental health to acknowledge and remember the anniversary of Aaron's death. A year following her son's death, an anniversary meal was arranged and attended by close family, friends and neighbours held at The Boars' Head Eatery, Birmingham in celebration of his life.

Joy would spend subsequent remembrance anniversaries listening to Aaron's favourite music, watch his favourite movies, and enjoy his favourite foods.

At Aaron's physical grave, Joy visits and takes bouquets of flowers as an act of remembrance to her son.

Joy also writes tribute posts to her loved one and publishes them on Aaron's Facebook page to mark his death anniversaries to acknowledge his anniversaries; commemorate the event because it is an opportunity to reconnect and re-affirm her life-long relationship with her son. It is Joy's time to give voice to her grief and sense of loss while at the very same time, learning to integrate Aaron's absence into her day-to-day life.

A Cry For Help

On Sunday 3rd January 2016, Aaron featured on the front page of *The Mirror* and *Sunday Mercury* Newspapers.

Newspaper reporter Mike Lockley wrote:

"Devastated Joy Lescott wants Health Secretary Jeremy Hunt to step in and investigate what caused the death of Aaron Jeffers.

Heartbroken: Joy Lescott is asking for help in examining the care of her son, Aaron received when he died in 2014, and has demanded help from the Government in solving the mystery of what killed her son.

Heartbroken Joy Lescott could only watch on as her sports-mad son Aaron Jeffers died in hospital after being admitted with a simple urine infection.

Joy could do nothing as her 23-year-old son deteriorated while a patient at Sandwell Hospital in West Bromwich, Birmingham.

According to the Birmingham Mail, Aaron, a top amateur footballer, was admitted to the hospital on October 24, 2013 after suffering stomach and back pain.

Despite medics' efforts, he declined rapidly, with his chest, hands and feet swelling grotesquely.

Medics were so concerned that Aaron was moved to the Queen Elizabeth Hospital in Edgbaston, Birmingham in December 2013.

He died on March 13 2014.

The fitness fanatic – a popular worker at ASDA's One Stop Shop in Perry Barr, Birmingham – had suffered two heart attacks and brain damage.

Fighting back tears, Primary School Teacher Joy recalled the last days of Aaron's life.

"You couldn't recognise Aaron," she said.

"His skin was charcoal grey; his eyes were lifeless, and his tongue was hanging out."

In the space of weeks, the frightened 49-year-old watched her son change from a carefree, popular individual to a bloated, bed-ridden patient all too aware that he was dying.

"We were never given a diagnosis," said Joy, from Kingstanding, Birmingham.

"We were never told why something we believed was simple and straightforward turned into this.

"Without knowing that, there can be no closure."

To Joy, who also has a 10 year-old son, Aaron's death remains a mystery.

There was no inquest, but Joy has called on Mr Hunt to order an independent investigation into the sequence of events that led to the tragedy.

Aaron, she said, voiced concerns about the care he received at Sandwell, although the hospital's own investigation found no failings in his treatment.

Joy said she wanted to know why Aaron was discharged 3 times by Sandwell Hospital, only to be taken back on the wards.

On one brief home visit, he asked to be taken to the ASDA One Stop Shop, Birmingham where he managed the self-service desk.

"His feet had swollen so much that it was difficult to lace up his shoes."

"Staff broke down in tears when they saw him."

"I realise now that he'd gone there to say goodbye."

"Aaron was the kindest, wittiest person you could wish to meet."

"No-one had a bad word to say about him."

"He adored his family and could do anything."

"He loved his music and he loved his football, yet at the end he looked like a 70 -year-old."

The countdown to the end of Aaron's life began on October 19, 2013, when he attended an NHS Walk-In Centre with back pain and breathing difficulties.

On his return, Aaron struggled to get out of his car and paramedics were called.

He was initially taken to Good Hope Hospital in Sutton Coldfield, Birmingham but discharged after 2 hours and given a course of antibiotics for a urine infection.

The drugs did not stem his decline.

On October 24 3013, Aaron was taken to Sandwell Hospital in West Bromwich, Birmingham and despite being placed on intravenous fluids, continued to slip rapidly. He was moved from the Emergency Assessment Unit to Intensive Care.

"He walked into that hospital," said Joy.

"We just can't understand how someone who walked into hospital didn't walk back out again."

"He couldn't even walk to the toilet."

Aaron was fitted with a catheter, but his body continued to swell alarmingly.

By November 2013, Joy realised her son was in a grim battle for life.

"I was in shock, I could not believe what was happening," she said.

"His body had swollen so much he looked like The Hulk," she added.

"On the day before his cardiac arrest, I could see in Aaron's eyes that he wanted me to leave."

"Looking good was very important to Aaron and he didn't want me to see him looking like that."

By December 9th 2013, Aaron's family was reduced to praying around his bed at the Queen Elizabeth Hospital, Birmingham.

"His hands and feet were cold," said Joy.

"I recited Psalms and said: 'I love you very much'. He was petrified and asked if he was going to die."

On December 10 2013, Joy was given the news her son had suffered cardiac arrests.

It was the beginning of a protracted end.

His life had been saved, but at a price.

Aaron had suffered brain damage and would never speak again.

Joy had effectively lost her son.

On March 13th 2014, Aaron died, the official cause being pneumonia, brain injury, cardiac arrest and Castleman's Disease, the medical terminology for multi-organ shutdown.

For Joy, the scars of watching her son's pitiful decline will never heal.

"I have to fight for my son," she told the Sunday Mercury.

"If I don't fight for my son, who will?"

In a letter to Health Secretary Jeremy Hunt, backed by local Community Activist, Desmond Jaddoo stated:

"Miss Lescott is still seeking answers as to why her son actually died. Aaron was a fit 23-year-old young man who had no previous bouts of illness and was an avid amateur footballer. Miss Lescott has shown me text message exchanges with her son where he revealed fears for his life. I would therefore urge your intervention in this matter and request an independent investigation into the death of Aaron Jeffers, which seeks to answer the questions being raised by his grieving mother."

Sandwell & West Birmingham Hospitals NHS Trust repeated its willingness to meet Aaron's family to discuss their concerns.

Chief Nurse Colin Ovington said: "Our condolences remain with Mr Jeffers' family and friends following his sad passing. We investigated the issues of complaint thoroughly and responded in April 2014 with a full report. We have not been contacted by Mr Jeffers' family since our response was sent but remain happy to meet to discuss any outstanding concerns. The evidence within our investigation indicates that our medical teams did all they could for Mr Jeffers."

When A Loved One Dies

Aaron and his mother were extremely close, like 2 peas in a pod and she mourned her beloved son. The remark "God knows best" came from well-meaning family and friends. However, Joy found these remarks more cutting than comforting. Aaron's death was not for the 'best,' she kept telling herself. It was clear that when Joy recounted when writing this book what had happened to her son years' later, she was still grieving.

As Joy came to see, it can take a long time for someone to overcome grief, especially when the bereaved person was very close to the deceased. The bible aptly describes death as 'the last enemy.' (1 Corinthians 15:26). It breaks into our lives with irresistible force, often when we are completely unprepared, and it robs us of those we hold dear. None of us are immune to is ravages. So, it is not surprising if we feel at a loss when it comes to coping with death, loss and its aftermath.

Maybe you have wondered: "How long does it take to get over grief? How can a person cope with grief? How can I comfort others who have been bereaved? Is there any hope for our loved ones who have died?

6 Years On

Aaron's life was very important. He took on challenges and inspired humanity. Now, Joy is telling her story. She has inspired herself and is passionate about inspiring others too! Remember those challenges you conquered? What about those problems, pain and trauma you solved? Someone else, somewhere on this planet needs to hear how you did those things.

They need to understand that it is possible, and that nothing is impossible. Impossible = (I'm possible). They need to be inspired by the way you conquered and solved them.

This book has really been for Joy's benefit – finding clarity, closure and a complete acceptance of what happened to her son. In other words, her ability to go beyond imposed limitations in order to find a different way to come to terms with her grief.

It has also given Joy a platform to provide her grandson with a legacy – her story about her son's life and the legacy that he left behind. It is that 'thing' that someone did either for 'better' or 'worse', and it is most often the 'thing' for which someone is most remembered.

This biography has been an account of 6 years Joy has been without her son's physical presence, and they have given her deep insight into her soul – a journey of self-discovery. This book has helped Joy to move through this phase of her life - and she can revisit them at any given time, as a reminder of her gradual development during bereavement.

"I realised the importance of reviewing my life, integrating my memories and making sense out of what I did and thought. Not only is it important to do this, it was also necessary and beneficial. When you review your life from start to present, you will encounter unresolved issues. Reviewing your life and accomplishments will force you to see how you have overcome real and perceived obstacles. Reflection can help you move past negative feelings of self-doubt, for example providing a path to perhaps a reconciliation in relationships with others.

Re-living your memories, writing down the facts and dates and events of your life and organising them together into a unified story with an interesting theme will require time, effort and persistence. As with any skill, the more you practice self-discipline the better you become at it. Increased self-discipline will help you in practically all areas of your life.

Perhaps as you reflect on your past aspirations or goals and your approach to life, you may find that you are not totally satisfied with what you see. There is still time to re-invent yourself by using your review to identify and move towards ways to reach that better you. As we reflect on our past, however, and find unfinished business or new goals to achieve, we can find renewed purpose for the remainder of our lives.

As you tell your story, you realise that your life had and has meaning and that at least some parts of it were well lived. As a result, you increase your own self esteem. Your satisfaction with yourself and your life will rise, and you should lose those continuous doubts about your own self-worth. Accept yourself as a valuable member of humanity. Your life is a canvas of colour. Colour it with your thoughts and feelings.

What have you been called to create in your life? Have I convinced you to write your autobiography?

Kwayme 6 Years On

"I don't know exactly what to say. All I know is my heart is breaking for you bro.

This is the second time I have expressed to you how I'm feeling since you passed, but the first time, I wrote you a song which is at the beginning of this

JOY M LESCOTT

book. The first one, I sung in my head a short while after you died. I know that you managed to either read, rap, hum or sing along to it because I know how much you love music.

It has been 6 years since I have not physically seen you, and that is the longest time I have gone without seeing you in the flesh, hearing your voice or watching your broad smile.

I was just 9 years old when mom told me you had died. We were both totally devastated and cried our eyes out. It was so sad to watch us crying over your absence, when all we wanted was to be in your existence. That day was the worst day of my life.

Instead, I visit you at your resting place, and that hurts so bad. It's no fun because I prefer to see you in person, as I was used to but know I can't, because I know you are not here. I must accept it – that's hard too.

Me and mom have been saying we are okay, but we're not fine really. One minute we are coping, then the next we aren't coping in our own unique way.

But we are getting better day by day as the pain of grief begins to ease. We keep ourselves busy so that our minds don't wonder.

I'm dealing with the loss of you, my brother, who I have known since day one. Mom tells me that when she gave birth to me and you came to see both of us in hospital, you could not wait to hold me. You reached out and held me in your loving arms whilst welcoming me in to the world. I know my entire family are also grieving the loss of you, but they may not truly understand the role you played in my life. So that is why it is important for me to communicate with them that I need their support. I know that I can also approach my family and friends when I need to. They will offer me the help that I need when I am feeling down about you, and they will re-assure me things will be okay and to remember you, my dear brother – always on my mind and forever in my heart.

I feel I have lost out on a long-term relationship with you, and the role I pictured you playing in my future. We had a deep connection with each other, like no other. We have been present in each other's lives through all our ups and downs. So, your death to me represents the loss of a friend, protector and someone who I trusted in to share many things. Everyone copes with the loss of a loved one differently. For me, I find ways to remember you through music to keep your memory alive and maintain that feeling of a deep connection with you.

Bro, it has been very difficult for me during this time, because I have not had a positive father figure to look up to. Mom does her best to play both roles as a parent, and I appreciate her for that. I just want you to know you have been a very positive influence and father figure to me since I was a baby and, I miss that. You showed me what being a man looks like. Without having this influence in my life, I am at risk of growing up into a man who has issues around emotional stability and relationships with others. I have always respected you for your fatherly trait, particularly when you used to have clear and consistent rules for me to follow. I did not appreciate it at the time, but it has taught me respect. I learned right from wrong with your calm words, actions and given consequences. Your emotional support helped to shape my identity and influenced my values when it came to my own beliefs about what is right and wrong.

The attention that you provided to me; your positive role modelling and the sense of belonging that you provided, all contributed to my development and sense of self-esteem.

Aaron, your presence in my life has kept me on the straight and narrow, making it less likely for me, as a young man to 'act out' and deal with my emotions.

As a father figure, you always showed active involvement in my education, which has helped me to gain better grades at school. Education is important because it teaches everyone, including children and young people how to speak and to write so that we can be the best people we can be. Education gives people the knowledge and skills that they need for success.

Big bro, I know that you are not here when I need a shoulder to cry on. That makes me sad. It's hard because you were my ride or die. But at least I have mom. Our loving mother, who I know I can rely on and approach for help, support or advice at any time. We both know, she has worked hard to make sure we were/are equipped with the knowledge, skills and abilities to make it as competent human beings. I love her for that, and I know you do too.

My successful brother has left a legacy and lessons behind for me to read in this book, as well as practice his advice, just like any other father figure.

I hope you are at peace now and free from pain and suffering. I also hope that I have made you extremely proud. I am trying my best − that's all you wanted me to do!"☺

Love you bro, Kwayme, aged 15. Will never forget you xx

Grandson's Poem, Dedicated To My Daddy 6 Years On

"It's been 6 years since my dear dad passed away,
I dedicate this to him and pray.
I cherish our past connection from conception we shared,
But will miss the future we will not have to pack
in an entire lifetime of love because we cared.

There are so many questions that I need answers to,
But now that you're gone there's no way to ask you.

But there are still photos to remember you by,
Each time I look at them, I still want to cry.

They say grief is easier to bear as time goes by,
But that doesn't stop me from wondering why?

Why my dear, sweet dad was taken so soon,
When he was my guiding star, my sun and my moon.

There are no answers to a question like this,
So, I'll treasure your memory, and mourn the years we'll miss.

Why Being A Parent After The Death Of A Parent Is Hard

People usually think of newly expectant mothers exploding with elation the moment they realise they are having a baby. The truth is that the idea of becoming a parent is often met with a mix of emotions that range from happiness to fear. Whether it is your first baby or your fifth, having a baby is a big deal and many people will long for the support of their partner, wife, boyfriend, husband or girlfriend as they begin this journey.

"Personally, something that I grieve repeatedly is the fact that my grandson will never know his father, and Aaron will never know his child. I think about how much they would have enjoyed each other, and it feels tragic to me that their lives never intersected."

No one likes to feel guilty, but sometimes you just cannot help it. It is hard to see your friend's parents show up for the football matches and celebrations for graduation and know that (a) this is something one of your parents never got to do and (b) your child will not have one of their parents around to cheer them on in life.

When you become a parent, you relive many of the experiences you had as a child, through your parents' eyes. This may cause you to think what it was like for your own parents when you were a child. It may give you a greater appreciation for the things they did for you and you may feel overwhelmed by old memories.

There is often a sadness felt, particularly when you cannot reach out to ask one of your parents a question about the past or to show your appreciation for them. This experience can be both painful and unpleasant. Experiencing childhood from an adult's perspective can allow you to feel connected with the memory of your parents in different ways, to feel grateful of everything they gave you, and to reflect on warm and comforting memories of the past.

Children can provide parents with a sense of purpose and joy when experiencing grief. Children sometimes say and do the funniest of things.

Being a parent allows you to connect with your loved one's memory in several different ways:

- Through the stories and memories, you share with your child(ren). You may love sharing stories with your child(ren) about your mother or father, just like you remember your mother or father sharing stories with you about their mother or father. Joy's grandson has never had the opportunity to meet his father, yet she knows her grandson knows so much about his father and the type of parent he was so looking forward to becoming.

- Through the traditions you carry on. When you carry on a tradition that was passed down to you by your parents, you will be creating the opportunity to connect with your memory of them, and to share the memory with your children.

- Through the lens of being a parent yourself. Being a parent allows you to connect with your parents in new ways. The relationships we have with our deceased loved ones do not get frozen in time. They continue to evolve and change. This means you may understand your parents in new ways at different ages of your life – when you were in your 20s, 30s, 40s and 50s etc.

Is It Wrong To Grieve?

Have you ever had a brief spell with illness? Perhaps you recovered so quickly that you have literally forgotten the sequence of events. Grief is not like that. There is no such thing as getting over grief. Over time and with the right support from others, your grief will soften.

As an example, consider the following of many who mourn the death of someone very close.

"My husband, Robert, died on 9th July 2008. The morning of the fatal accident was no different from any other day.

After breakfast, as we always did when he was leaving for work, we gave each other a kiss, a cuddle, and an 'I love you.' 6 years later the pain in my heart is still there. I do not think I will ever get over my loss of Rob." Grace, aged 60.

"Although I have been without my dear wife for more than 18 years, I still miss her and grieve over my loss. Whenever I see something in nature that is attractive, my thoughts go to her, and I cannot help wondering how she would have enjoyed seeing what I am seeing." Evan aged 84.

Clearly, such painful and long-lasting feelings are only natural. Each person will grieve in his or her own way, and it would be unfair to judge the way another person responds to tragedy.

Dealing With Your Grief

There is no shortage of advice on this subject, but not all of it however is helpful. You may find that some will advise you not to cry or show your feelings. Others may push you to do the opposite and expose all your feelings.

Mental health experts acknowledge that tearfulness is a normal part of the grieving process. Grieving may, in time, help you to move on despite the enormity of your loss. Suppressing grief, however, will do more harm than good.

The pain one experiences when they lose a loved one can be unbearable. Understandably, grief is very complex and complicated, and we sometimes wonder if the pain will ever go away. The bereaved go through a variety of emotional experiences such as anger, confusion, and sadness. Learning about emotions after a loss can help us to heal.

Did you know that when we lose a loved one, we go through 5 distinct stages of grief after the loss of a loved one? Denial, anger, bargaining, depression, and finally acceptance.

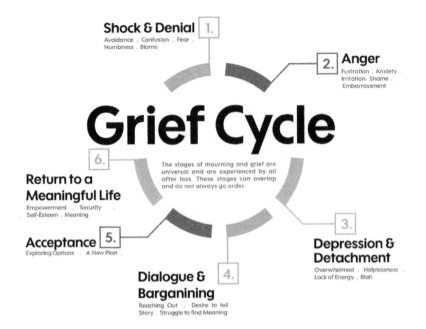

Grief Cycle

1. **Shock & Denial**
Avoidance . Confusion . Fear . Numbness . Blame

2. **Anger**
Fustration . Anxiety . Irritation. Shame . Embarrassment

3. **Depression & Detachment**
Overwhelmed . Helplessness . Lack of Energy . Blah

4. **Dialogue & Barganining**
Reaching Out . Desire to tell Story . Struggle to find Meaning

5. **Acceptance**
Exploring Options . A New Plan .

6. **Return to a Meaningful Life**
Empowerment . Security . Self-Esteem . Meaning

The stages of mourning and grief are universal and are experienced by all after loss. These stages can overlap and do not always go order.

Denial

The first stage of loss is denial. Denial can help us to block out the overwhelming pain of loss. As we try to process the reality of our loss, we are also trying to survive emotional pain. It can be hard to believe we have lost an important person or loved on in our lives, especially when we may have just spoken with this person the previous week or even the previous day. Our reality shifts completely in that moment of loss. It can take our minds some time to adjust to this new reality.

Denial is not only an attempt to pretend that the loss does not exist, but we are also trying to absorb and understand what is happening, all at the same time.

We begin reflecting on experiences we have shared with the person we lost, and we might find ourselves wondering how we are going to move forward in our life without this person. This is a lot of information to explore and a lot of painful imagery to process.

Anger

It is very common for people to experience bouts of anger after the loss of a loved one, especially in cases of sudden, unexpected death because we are trying to adjust to a new reality. At this stage anger forces us to experience extreme emotional discomfort.

Unfortunately, anger is the first thing we feel when we start to release emotions related to loss. Very often we begin to blame others for our loss. This leaves us feeling isolated in our experience, perceived by others as unapproachable in moments when we could benefit from comfort, connection, and re-assurance.

What about guilt? Especially in the case of unexpected death, the bereaved person may repeatedly think, 'It might not have happened if only I had done this or that.'

Or maybe your last encounter with the deceased involved an argument. This may add to your feelings of guilt. If you are being pestered with such feelings of guilt and anger, it is important not to bottle up these emotions. Instead, speak to a friend or someone you can confide in who will listen and re-assure you that such irrational feelings are common to many bereaved ones. A true friend always shows love and is someone who you can rely on in times of distress. The best friend a bereaved person can have is our Creator, Jehovah God. Pour out your heart to him in prayer because 'he cares for you'. (1 Peter 5:7). Jehovah God promises that all who do so will have their thoughts and feelings soothed by 'the peace of God that surpasses all understanding.' (Philippians 4:6, 7). Allow God to help you heal by means of his consoling word, the bible. Joy said that at times she felt intense loneliness. But she has found help in prayer. *"When I pray to Jehovah God as encouraged by my mother,"* she explains, *"I never feel alone. After reading and meditating on comforting thoughts from The Watchtower and then in my most difficult times, breaking down in tears and pouring out the feelings in my heart in prayer, I sense a calmness and a transcending peace come over me, putting my mind and heart at rest and enabling me to carry on and take one day at a time. Jehovah God listened to my prayers and always gives me strength when I need it."*

Some Bereavement Counsellors advise those who are struggling with grief to get involved in helping others or to volunteer their time in some community service, as doing so can bring joy and may ease a person's grief.

Bargaining

It is common that when coping with loss to feel so desperate that you are willing to do almost anything to alleviate or lessen the pain. Losing a loved one can cause us to consider any way we can to avoid the current pain or the pain we are expecting from loss.

When bargaining starts to take place, we often direct our requests to a higher power, or something bigger than we are that may be able to influence change to our situation. Then in these moments, we realise there is nothing we can do to influence change or a better outcome. This feeling of helplessness can cause us to react in protest by bargaining, which gives us a perceived sense of control over something that feels so out of control.

While bargaining we also tend to focus on our personal faults or regrets. We might look back at our interactions with the person we are losing and reflect on all the times we felt disconnected or may have caused them pain. It is common to recall times when we may have said hurtful things we did not mean and wish we could go back and change and behave differently. We also tend to make the drastic assumption that if we had treated others differently, we would not be in such an emotionally painful place in our lives.

Depression

During the grieving process, there comes a time when our imaginations calm down and we slowly start to look at the reality of our present situation. Bargaining no longer feels like an option and we are faced with reality - what is currently happening. It is at this stage that we begin to feel the loss of our loved one.

As our panic begins to subside, the emotional fog begins to clear, and the loss feels more present and unavoidable. In those moments, we tend to pull inward as the sadness grows. We might find ourselves retreating, being less sociable, living the life of a recluse, and reaching out less to others about what we are going through. Although this is a very natural stage of grief, dealing with depression after the loss of a loved one can be extremely isolating.

Acceptance

When we come to a place of acceptance, it is not that we no longer feel the pain of loss. However, we are no longer resisting the reality of our situation, and we are not struggling to make it something different. Sadness and regret can still be present in this phase, but the emotional survival tactics of denial, bargaining, and anger is less present.

Types of Grief

Looking at the 5 stages of grief, it is important to note that people grieve differently, and we may or may not go through each of these stages, or experience each of them in order. The lines of these stages are often blurred—we may move from one stage to the other and possibly back again before fully moving into a new stage.

In addition, there is no specific time period suggested for any of these stages.

Someone may experience the stages quickly, such as in a matter of weeks, where another person may take months or even years to move through to a place of acceptance. Whatever time it takes for you to move through these stages is perfectly normal.

Your pain is unique to you, your relationship to the person you lost is unique, and the emotional processing can feel different to each person. It is acceptable for you to take the time you need and remove any expectation of how you should be feeling as you process your grief.

Comforting Those Who Mourn

Have you ever felt helpless when someone near to you was grieving over the loss of a loved one? Sometimes we may feel unsure about what to say or do – so we end up saying or doing nothing.

There are practical, helpful things we can do to help the bereaved. Often all that is needed is your presence, together with a simple expression such as "I am sorry" or giving the person a hug or a gentle squeeze of the arm is an effective way to show you care. If the bereaved one wants to talk, listen sympathetically. Best of all, do something for the bereaved family, such as performing a chore the grieving one has not been able to care for, for example cooking a meal, caring for the children or helping with funeral arrangements if that is the family's wish. Such actions may speak louder than the most eloquent words.

In time, you may be moved to talk about the deceased, focusing on some good qualities or happy experiences. Such conversations may even bring a smile to the bereaved person's face. For example, AJ's mother says: *"People sometimes tell me good things that Aaron did that I never knew about, and that makes my heart feel good."*

On reflection Aaron's mother reports: *"I received a lot of initial help after Aaron passed, but my needs were soon forgotten as friends got busy again with their own lives."* Therefore, make a point of contacting a bereaved friend on a regular basis after the loss.

Some have even marked the date of the death on their calendar as a reminder to offer comfort when it may be most needed – on or near the date of the loss. Many grieving ones deeply appreciate this opportunity to relieve themselves of prolonged feelings of grief. There are many ways we can offer practical help and comfort to those who mourn. The bible also comforts us by means of a thrilling hope for the future.

Avoid Rescuing Or Fixing

It can be so difficult to know what to say to someone who has experienced loss. We do our best to offer comfort, but sometimes our best efforts can feel inadequate and unhelpful to the bereaved person. One thing to remember is that the person who is grieving does not need to be fixed. In our attempts to be helpful, we tend to try to rescue people from their pain so they will feel better. We provide uplifting, hopeful comments or even try to offer them humour to help ease their pain. Although the intention is positive, this approach can leave people feeling as if their pain is not seen, heard, or valid.

Don't Force It

Another method people often use that tends to go wrong is forcing people to talk about their pain when they are not ready. We want so much to help and for the person to feel better, so we believe that nudging them to talk and process their emotions will help them faster. This is not necessarily true, and it can be an obstacle to their healing. Talking about pain is the best remedy, but only when the person going through the pain is ready to talk.

Make Yourself Accessible

One of the most helpful things we can do is to offer space for people to grieve. In doing this, we are letting the person know that we are available and accessible when they are ready to talk. We can invite them to talk with us but remember to provide understanding and validation if they are not ready to talk just yet. At that point, you can remind them that you are available when they feel ready and not to hesitate to come to you.

A Word From Someone Who Has Lost A Loved One

It is important to remember that everyone copes with loss differently. While you may find that you experience all 5 stages of grief, you may also find that it is difficult to classify your feelings into any one of the stages. Have patience with yourself and your feelings in dealing with loss. Allow yourself time to process all of your emotions, and when you are ready to speak about your experiences with loved ones or a healthcare professional, do so. If you are supporting someone who has lost a loved one, remember that you do not need to do anything specific, but allow them room to talk about it when they are ready.

How To Look After Yourself

The period following bereavement will undoubtedly be hard, but there are things that you can do to look after yourself.

Talk About Your Feelings

Talk to someone you trust about your feelings, such as a partner, a close friend or family member.

Talk About The Person

Do not be afraid to talk about the person who has died like you used to when they were alive, because not mentioning them can leave you feeling isolated and alone in your grief.

Allow Yourself To Feel Emotions

If you feel sad and need to cry, let it out. It is important to grieve for your loved one and crying can help to release these emotions. If you feel angry, try and release this emotion in a safe way, or try journaling to write down and release your emotions.

Take Care Of Yourself

Try as much as possible to eat a healthy, balanced diet, get enough sleep (or rest if you cannot sleep) and exercise.

Maintain Your Social Life

It is easy to feel like you do not want to do anything when you are grieving, however, it is important to continue your hobbies and meeting up with good friends. Maintaining your routine and social life will help distract you or make you feel better, even if for a short time.

Avoid Short-Term Fixes

Avoid relying on alcohol or taking drugs as these do not solve anything. These will only mask over the pain you will be feeling and can make you feel worse in the long-term.

Allow Yourself To Adjust

Losing someone close to you is incredibly hard. Accept that you may need to adjust to living on your own or learn how to do tasks normally done by the person you lost, such as cooking, DIY or finances.

Do not be afraid to ask for help if you need it.

Do What You Can On Special Occasions

Anniversaries and special occasions can be really hard when you are missing a loved one, so do whatever you need to do to get through them. This might mean taking time off work, going away somewhere or spending time with others you care about to distract yourself. The first occasions without your loved one, (e.g. birthdays, Christmas), will always be the hardest, so ask a good friend or family member to be there with you if possible.

Life will not be the same after losing your loved one, but in time you will create a new normality. Many people find that the bad days eventually become fewer and fewer, and they can still miss the person they lost while also regaining their enjoyment in life.

Religion & Grief

When someone we love dies, it is inevitable that questions of faith and spirituality arise. For some faith is challenged, for others it is a no-go area, for some it is a great comfort, and for some it is a new exploration.

"I believe we are all spiritual beings, although formal religious belief may not be a part of our life. Regardless, tending to the spiritual side is a part of the

healing process, and I have found these following bible verses helpful in supporting the spiritual side of my grief journey, offering me hope." explains Joy.

What The Bible Says

Revelation 21:3, 4 reads *"Jehovah God himself will be with them. And he will wipe every tear from their eyes, and death will be no more, neither will mourning nor outcry nor pain be anymore. The former things have passed away."*

"There is going to be a resurrection."—Acts 24:15.

What That Can Mean For You

Comfort when loved ones die. —2 Corinthians 1:3, 4.

Freedom from a morbid fear of death. —Hebrews 2:15.

A real hope of being reunited with your dead loved ones. —John 5:28, 29.

Can We Really Believe What The Bible Really Says?

Yes, for at least 3 reasons: God is the Creator of life. The Bible calls Jehovah God 'the source of life'. (Psalm 36:9; Acts 17:24, 25) The One who gave life to all living creatures is certainly capable of restoring life to someone who has died.

Jehovah God has resurrected humans in the past. The Bible reports 8 instances of humans—young, old, male, and female—who were brought back to life on earth. Some had been dead for a short while, but one had been in a tomb for 4 days! (John 11:39-44).

God is eager to do it again. Jehovah hates death; he views it as an enemy. (1 Corinthians 15:26) He has a longing to conquer that enemy, to undo death by means of the resurrection. He yearns to bring back those who are in his memory and to see them live on earth again (Job 14:14, 15).

Aaron's grandmother acts in harmony with her beliefs, sharing with Aaron's mother, family and the local community Jehovah God's promise of a future when 'death will be no more'.

If you have ever suffered the loss of someone dear to you, this information may not completely take away your grief. By meditating on Jehovah God's promises found in the bible, you can find real hope and the strength to keep going (1 Thessalonians 4:13).

Encouraging people to be honest about their struggles with (or without) faith is such a re-assuring thing to do.

"In times of need, try and draw close to Jehovah God and ask him for comfort and guidance. When we make a commitment to have a relationship and get to know God and obey him, he is there for us. Pain will always enter our lives, but Jehovah God is our Comforter." writes Joy.

Faith and/or spirituality are a part of life and contribute to our mental health and ability to survive hardship. However, spirituality takes form in your beliefs, embrace it for yourself, and nurture it in others, as they seek peace and comfort at such critical times in life.

Finding Your Way After Losing A Loved One

Joy had several milestone events that occurred during and after her son's bout of illness. She suffered with intense pain in her body when she was visiting her sick son in hospital care for 5 months.

The author became diagnosed with Vitamin D Deficiency and Diabetes soon after her son died. Living with an invisible illness is hard to explain to someone who has no idea of the daily struggles you face. Feeling pain; putting on a brave face for everyone. There are many forms of invisible illnesses – Chrone's PTSD, Anxiety, Depression, Diabetes, Lupus, Fibromyalgia, MS, ME, Arthritis, Cancer, Heart Disease, Epilepsy, Autism, Alzheimer's and many other types of invisible illnesses coped with daily.

Aaron's mother turned 50, 2 years after he passed away and has misses her son's birthday greetings and wishes each and every year thereafter.

Joy also became a grandmother for the very first time, but she deeply missed not having her son there by her side to see him fulfil his greatest wish, which was to be the best dad ever to his first born.

If you ignore grief and push it down, you can live and you can even function, but you will live a very narrow emotional life because you are using so much emotional energy to cope.

Everything in your psyche will be squashed down, and that means small things can trigger a much bigger kind of effect. The fact is you must do the work of grieving. You must let it run its course. Pain is the agent of change; pain is what allows you to change, it is what enables you to reach a new reality.

What have you stopped doing since experiencing the death of your loved one? More specifically, what do you no longer do that you used to previously enjoy or find fulfilling?

Now, what if I told you that by deliberately deciding to do these things again one step at a time, or by choosing new things to try, that you might start to feel a little bit better? Or that by doing these things you are, in many ways, coping with your grief?

By doing new things, you may feel a sense of mastery or fulfilment, allowing you to feel calm and at peace, increase your physical well-being, or simply help you to feel human again.

If you have cut out activities that used to be an important part of your life, things that had inherent value, then it may be time for you to schedule them back in. Plan and consider what other positive/constructive/therapeutic activities you could begin to work into your schedule. Are there coping tools you would like to try? Are there ways you want to honour and remember your loved one?

After you have taken stock of your schedule and the types of activities that are missing from your life, schedule them back in. It may help you to ask others to keep you accountable. Talk to your family or friends about your plans and ask them to ask you how it went next time they see you.

Do not give in to your excuses, rationalisations, or reasons why not. If you are sceptical, then prove yourself wrong. In other words, just try it and see. While engaging in the activity, or taking up a new interest, pay attention to how you are feeling.

After someone dies, some of your most valued and fulfilling experiences are often coloured with a tinge of pain. Part of coping with grief is learning to tolerate and work through painful emotions, so prepare to feel frustrated and to doubt yourself and to feel all sorts of emotion, but please believe it is worth it in the end.

After A Loved One Passes Away

Joy writes *"I became 'anxious, nervous and extremely depressed' after my son, Aaron passed away in 2014. I was aware that many future moments would be consumed by vast emptiness."* She did not know how to stop her dive into the depths of despair, as she missed her son and tried to make sense of the loss.

"He has really gone, period." She was still here but fading away.

"It will never be the same again." Joy says she looks at her second born and grandson and counts her blessings for that – and she does too.

"You never recapture what you had. I am not down, you come to terms with the loss and you learn to live with it, and you must move on, or you make yourself ill. When you have got a child and other dependents you cannot afford to do that because you have got someone else who depends on you. You cannot just give up. That would be so selfish."

Although Joy did not have any friends at the time that had lost a son or daughter, she has since encountered several people who have lost a child. They too could identify with feelings of emptiness, isolation, numbness and depression. They did not know how they could go on, how they would survive, how they would handle the pain or how they could make the pain go away.

"You may recall Aaron, just before you became ill, I was studying at home. I had to put my studying on hold to support you through your sickness. After you passed away, I decided to pluck up the strength and courage to finish what I started, as I know that is what you would have wanted me to do. I can hear you right now "Did you finish your studying, and did you pass?" I just want to let you know that I am so proud of myself for gaining a Level 4 Diploma in Higher Level Teaching whilst going through a very tough time in my life. I am now working in the Project Management arena. I know you would have been very proud of me – you showed and expressed that to me often enough."

For Joy, starting the transition back to work was 'a saviour, a chance to feel useful and connected.' When she returned to work, she realised 'relationships with my co-workers had changed – I knew why, they wanted to help me but were not sure how. Should I talk about it? Should I not talk about it? If I talked about it, what the hell do I say? People do not know what to say or how to react. They do not want to remind you of your sad loss. There is no solution and that frightens people too. They can find it frustrating and do not know what to do. It is a strange reminder of how fragile life can be and it suddenly hits home that it can happen to them.'

Eventually, she knew she could not go on feeling vulnerable, anxious and depressed indefinitely. For Joy, it helped to admit that she was vulnerable and invited her co-workers to talk about it. *"Speaking openly replaced the fear in my co-workers of doing and saying the wrong thing,"* she writes.

"Because I was in a teaching role, going through loss when I was teaching had its own set of unique challenges. Teaching is stressful by itself, so when you add the extra layer of loss, it can seem unbearable for a Teacher to want to return to the classroom and face 30 children every day. You will rarely know when a Teacher is struggling because once they walk through those classroom doors, they put their own hardships behind them and focus on the many complex needs of the 30 eager minds in front of them – and that is their real superpower. Going through such hard loss myself has taught me so much about life and helping others through grief."

Benefits Of Volunteering

As part of Joy's volunteering experience, she shares her personal story as a Children's Rights Advocate - one of her amazing achievements.

She represented one of the more diverse and challenging volunteering roles within the Birmingham Local Authority's Children's Services, where she provided a high level of support to children and young people who had the status of being 'looked after' whilst Aaron was attending primary school.

It all began when Joy was approached by a Children's Rights Officer shortly after a Children's Rights Day Event to set up and run focus groups specifically for the needs of 'looked after' children and young people from black and minority ethnic backgrounds – something she had never undertaken before. Joy felt the role sounded very beneficial to help these vulnerable children and young people (now adults and parents), and the rest is history.

Many 'looked after' children have previous experiences of violence, abuse or neglect. Often, they display behavioural problems and attachment difficulties (problems forming secure relationships) which are associated with their negative life experiences. This means that some find it hard to develop positive peer and adult relationships.

"Empowerment is important for all children and young people. It is particularly important for 'looked after' children because they often report feeling powerless when decisions are made that affect their lives, or who experience a lack of stability in their care journey, including frequent changes in the professionals who support them and the adults who care for them," said Joy.

What Joy enjoyed the most about advocacy was ensuring the views, wishes, experiences and feelings of children and young people in her care was heard and considered when decisions were made about their future and lives.

A highlight of Joy's volunteering took place on the day of Aaron's funeral:

"It was at Aaron's burial and to my surprise that a number of these (then children and young people) - now adults, parents, authors, live presenters on on-line business/talk shows and who attended the monthly focus groups I had facilitated when they were just 13 years old were stood right by my side, including Advocates (Corinne Ellis, Sarah Fergus and Steven Richards) offering me emotional and moral support at a time when I was going through the toughest time of my life. I guess they believed I had made a difference to their lives, and now they wanted to give something back.

My parents always encouraged me to do good and good will follow you – and they were right. Those groups of adults and parents, who attended the focus groups in my care when they were 13 years old and who attended Aaron's funeral meant so much to me. It showed me how much they respected me and loved Aaron too. It was good for me to see representatives of the focus groups again, so grown up, independent and mature – you all inspire me. We indulged in enjoyable recollections of past focus group events - sharing 'silly things and quirks.' This boosted my inner strength, cheering me up and making me laugh a little. Today, 6 years on, we are still very much in touch with each other, chilling out and catching up over regular meals out, enjoying each other's company."

Here are tips that eased me through my grief:

Educate Yourself

The 5 stages of grief mentioned earlier: denial, anger, bargaining, depression, and acceptance helps all of us have common language around grief but remember that the stages of grief are not a linear, step-by-step experience. You do not go through these stages one after another. Grief is different for every single person and grief changes over time.

Take time to read and educate yourself about grief - I recommend identifying and understanding your feelings. It can help you process your loss as well as communicate your needs to others.

Ask Questions That Encourage Reflection On His/Her Reactions To Grief

- Do you feel like talking?
- How do you feel?
- Are you eating OK?
- Are you getting out of the house and engaging in your normal activities, conversation and hobbies?
- How have things been with your family and friends?
- Is anything bothering you lately?
- Can you tell me about your loved one?
- What about other difficult times in your life?
- Were these recent or in the past?
- What coping skills have you used in past crisis?
- When I was going through a difficult time, something I tried was 'X'... do you think this could help you?
- What can I do to help?

Provide Tangible Support & Tactical Encouragement

- Offer the survivor practical assistance – shop for groceries or run errands, cooking, housework or accompany them on a walk.

- Help the bereaved person acknowledge past accomplishments as a way of re-establishing self-esteem.

- Ask about his/her relationship with the deceased.

- Help him/her identify feelings of loss and feel pain. Acknowledge that pain is a part of the grief experience; re-assure him/her the pain will not always be so intense.

- Remind the survivor that it is normal to feel overwhelmed by the intensity of his/her feelings.

- Help him/her identify feelings of loss and feel pain. Acknowledge that pain is a part of the grief experience; re-assure him/her the pain will not always be so intense.

- Give him/her permission to cry—and permission to feel relieved if he/she does experience relief.

- Acknowledge that setbacks do happen and remind him/her not to panic. Grief can feel like an emotional roller coaster at times, but explain that these are remnants of grief, not a signal that it is starting all over again.

- Grief is physically and emotionally exhausting.

- Encourage the bereaved to take care of themselves by eating balanced meals, drinking plenty of water, getting enough sleep, exercising regularly and limiting alcohol and other mind-altering drugs, all of which can hinder the grief process.

- Encourage self-patience and patience with others who might not understand their feelings.

- Remind him/her to have realistic expectations about the amount of time required to heal from grief.

- Encourage him/her to take one day at a time. At times, it might be easier to break the day into manageable chunks.

- Encourage him/her to do small things for other people to refocus attention from their own pain.

- Re-assure him/her that it is okay to set limits with others and say *"no"* when appropriate.

- Affirm his/her right to feel joy, hope and new relationships— none of which are disloyal to the person who has died.

Utilise These Specific Aids With The Bereaved

Some bereaved feel the need, especially right after a death, to find out everything they can about the illness and/or circumstance of their loved one's death, and sometimes they want to review the medical records. This is normal and especially typical in a sudden death.

- Encourage the use of symbols and 'transitional objects' such as photos, audio or video tapes, articles of clothing or jewellery, or a collection that was special to the deceased.

- Suggest expressing his/her thoughts or feelings by writing a letter to the deceased or God.

- Suggest keeping a journal, poems or special remembrances of the grief experience.

- Suggest the use of art work, memory books, memory boxes and the like to express their grief feelings.

- If he/she has 'unfinished business' with the person who died, encourage him/her to play out in his/her mind what the issue is and how it could have been resolved. Focusing on what the survivor was able to do for the deceased, rather than what he/she should have done—can support recovery.

- Encourage him/her to role-play situations they fear or feel awkward about, such as starting a new relationship or selling a house. Role-playing can build stronger coping skills.

- Encourage the survivor to join a support group. Grief can feel very lonely, even when you have loved ones around. Sharing your sorrow with others who have experienced similar losses can help.

To find a Bereavement Support Group in your area, contact local hospitals, hospices, funeral homes, and counselling centres.

Watch For Warning Signs Of Depression

It is very common for a grieving person to feel depressed, confused, disconnected from others, or like they are going crazy.

But if the bereaved person's symptoms do not gradually start to fade, or their symptoms get worse with time, this is a sign that normal grief has evolved into a more serious problem, such as depression.

Encourage the grieving person to seek professional help if you observe any of the following warning signs after the initial grieving period, especially if it has been over a few months since the death.

- Difficulty functioning in daily life.

- Extreme focus on the death.

- Excessive bitterness, anger, or guilt.

- Neglecting personal hygiene.

- Alcohol or drug abuse.

- Inability to enjoy life.

- Withdrawing from others.

- Constant feelings of hopelessness.

- Talking about dying or suicide.

It can be extremely tricky to bring up your concerns to the bereaved person as you do not want to be perceived as invasive. It can be extremely tricky to bring up your concerns to the bereaved person as you do not want to be perceived as invasive. Instead of telling the person what to do, try expressing your own feelings: *"I am troubled by the fact that you are not sleeping or eating, perhaps you should look into getting help."*

Kids Will Push You Into Tomorrow

Many times when people experience loss, they want to crawl into a hole and isolate themselves. But when you are a Teacher, which Joy was, you are expected to go back to work rather quickly.

"Going back to the classroom after losing Aaron was something I was dreading. I was so tired and sad. I barely had anything to give my own second born, so how was I going to give to a classroom of 30 students? Something magical happened when I returned to school. Those students pushed me into tomorrow. Once I got back to school, they gave my life structure and purpose. They needed me. I needed them. I missed them. They loved me. I loved them. They missed me. They hugged me. I hugged them back. They made me laugh. They saw me cry. They saw me struggle. I talked to them about my grief. I had such a special bond with the students I supported. Those little people helped me come to life again," Joy wrote.

Lean into your students or the people who love you and let them help you come back to life. If you let them in, they will push you into tomorrow.

Find Your People

Here is the truth: people are going to let you down. There are people that are completely paralysed by death and so uncomfortable by the thought of speaking to a grieving person that they do nothing. Do not waste your time thinking about the people that do nothing. Instead focus on the people you can count on because you are going to need them. You are going to need them for hundreds of reasons and for a long time. One of the best things you can do for yourself is to figure out the people who will support you and then communicate your needs to them. Simply say, *"I'm going to need you. I trust you and I am going to need your help to make it through this."* People so badly want to help in your time of need, so utilise them and do not be afraid to ask for help.

About your support system - you may be surprised who shows up during your time of need. Lean on those who have experienced a few tough things in their life - you may earn a new, wise and true friend out of your hardship.

For all of you going through loss, I know first-hand how hard it will be. You will never be the same again, but Joy can re-assure you that you will find your new normal.

How Writing Can Help Grief &

How It Can Help You

So, Joy took the following steps to begin to move her life forward. Here are a few things she found useful:

Writing & Reading Is Your Best Friend

Joy wrote: *"Grief turned me into an emotional and depressed state, which made me feel helpless."*

This is a common experience. As anybody who has been there will know, one of the most surprising things about grief is how alone it makes you feel. Only those who have grieved will be able to understand what you are going through. Your friends and family will offer as much comfort as they can give, but they have got their own lives to live and nobody wants to hear your sorrowful story repeatedly.

"Writing provided me with comfort and relief at a time when nothing else did. I lived remotely and did not want to see a Therapist," Joy said.

"This book (then manuscript) became my lifesaver and my best friend. It was the only place where I could speak my truth and where I could safely express all my feelings, emotions, concerns and fears. It was always there for me to listen to the same story, over and over again, without judgement, until I was finally ready to let it go." Joy said.

"Your willingness to look at your darkness is what empowers you to change" - Iyanla Vanzant.

Joy has read a lot of self-help books. Most books she has read have been very helpful and have had many brilliant ideas and actionable takeaways that she applied to her daily life.

Here is what she has gained from being a personal development and self-help devotee for most of her adult life.

Some of the best-selling books of our time are self-help books. While some people lose themselves in advice, suggestions and routines, they also lose sight that in order to succeed or improve in any area of your life, you need to do something. There is nothing wrong with advice, however unless you are using it to do something it does not count as anything.

Others feel self-help books do not work because they must be the ones who takes responsibility for their current state and implement changes in their life. They need to decide how the concepts they read about will work given their circumstances and surroundings. The book can change their perspective, but they must change their life.

Joy shares her top 3 most meaningful lessons she has learned from diving into reading self-help books and applying knowledge in to her life, which made her feel better. Being able to learn from the successes and mistakes of others is an incredible asset.

A great way to materialise your knowledge is to share it with others. Rephrasing what you know and then publicising it gives you a public record of your thoughts and can highlight areas where you still need growth. Talking over these changes with a Counsellor or Therapist if you wish is a great way to jump-start your journey towards success. As a bonus, speaking to others about your journey of self-development gives them permission to start theirs. Be the light that sets the world aflame with the passion needed to create positive change. When you embody that which you wish to become, you align your attention with your intention and achieve your dreams. The key to life is not being a passive user of knowledge, it is implementing what you learn and creating something new. The more that you learn, implement, and create, the better your world becomes.

Lesson 1: Stop Avoiding Pain & Discomfort

We, the human species, are addicted to happiness. We crave happiness but avoid the hazards and sorrows at all costs.

"What I discovered through my self-help book journey is that, the secret to being happy is doing the opposite. Instead of avoiding unhappiness, strive to embrace uncomfortable emotions. Feel them, approach them, really dive into them head first. When those feelings get enough attention, and are exhausted, only then will you feel at peace. Repressing, suppressing, or reflectively reacting to uncomfortable feelings does not rid you of them. It makes you bitter, angry, short fused and you begin to bottle things up. What worked is accepting pain and discomfort as part of me, giving them space to exist, and feeling them fully.

I have learned to love and welcome the discomfort when it shows up. I see it as an opportunity to learn something about myself; to be true to myself so that I can be true to others; to self-love; to discover a feeling that I have repressed for a long time, or to have a good cry and let something out that I have been holding inside for too long. To be free again, we need to break through the discomfort by accepting it, giving it space, loving it, and eventually letting it go."

Here are the books that helped Joy shape this process for herself:

Peace From Broken Pieces is about the lessons our soul is designed to learn. It is not a book only about the author and spiritual healer Iyanla Vanzant, but a universal story of hurts and wounds, of denials and betrayal, lies and truth... but above all the light of Jehovah God that makes us rise above it and make us shine.

'One Day My Soul Just Opened Up' is a programme of inspiration and motivation that will help you work through problems and improve your emotional and spiritual health. Through exercises and readings, Iyanla Vanzant provides you with the tools to tap into your strengths and make your dreams come true.

Yesterday I Cried - bestselling author Iyanla Vanzant has had an amazing and difficult life - one of great challenges that unmasked her wonderful gifts and led to wisdom gained. In this simple book, she uses her own personal experiences to show how life's hardships can be re-languaged and re-visioned to become lessons that teach us as we grow, heal, and learn to love. The pain of the past does not have to be today's reality. Iyanla Vanzant is an example of how yesterday's tears become the seeds of today's hope, renewal, and strength.

Lesson 2: There Is A Reason For How Things Are

"Everything in our life happens for a reason." A familiar saying that everyone of us hears during difficult and challenging times throughout of our lives. We may not understand at the time why such things happen, however as time goes on, the answers as to why we experience certain things in our lives become apparent.

The thought that everything happens for a reason can be comforting to people especially when experiencing adversity. Joy truly started believing it.

It is a phrase we all particularly and naturally gravitate to when life gets a little too hard.

Here is why:

"I can approach all experiences I go through, good and bad, as a learning opportunity."

"There is purpose, meaning and growth to be gained from whatever tough times I face. All of life's challenges are there to offer me growth and insights to help me rise up stronger and higher as my mightiest self."

"The truth is my grieving situation felt dire, but the time came when I had to accept my loss and move on."

"I did not realise at the time of my loss that the purpose of my life did not depend on my son. Just because Aaron was the meaning of my life for so long does not mean that he must remain that way for the rest of my life. (This may sound harsh.) Just as I assigned the meaning of my life to my son, I decided to turn my tragic situation and re-assign it to something positive, so I decided to write this book. The meaning of my life and the reason why I wanted to keep going was not just an idea."

"The inspiration my son gave me for writing this book felt like there was another living entity that existed within me that needed to be reborn. It is a part of who I am, my body and soul, and its co-ordinates with the things I think and feel. It is a deep part of you that you are not even aware of sometimes. That is the power you can have. This is how dynamic you can truly be."

"For a while, I completely gave up on my search for a purpose. Then I discovered by reflecting on my life that my purpose showed up through my actions whenever I helped others. I just shifted my perspective, from what I can take from life today, to how I can contribute to life today."

When you start living your purpose, you reach your place in existence. You start understanding that you belong to life, and you are an active part of it. Then you find fulfilment and start being grateful for the things in your life.

"I would not wish tragedy upon anyone. However, I found the reality is the most tragic moments in our lives are the ones that define us the most. Our most tragic moments bring our greatest opportunities, if we have the courage to seize them."

"You may feel like you cannot find any reasons to keep on living. You have lost that thing that gave you purpose and drive. You have lost your passion for life. But you are starting to feel a flicker of light within."

"You can see that you have been giving up your power by defining your reasons for living based on other people, other relationships or other things outside yourself. You are now starting to see that your reasons for living can come from small acts of kindness. You can discover a purpose that has always existed inside you. You can also see that the obstacles you face can be your greatest opportunity, if you accept responsibility and do not shy away from it. If this even resonates just a little, congratulations. You are going through a very important shift in perspective."

"This slight shift in awareness holds great potential for planting a seed within that will slowly grow and start to move you forward in life."

"It is now your responsibility to nurture this seed, to continually remind yourself of the gift of life that you and many other people around you have. The truth is this: You owe it to yourself to continue nurturing this seed within. You just need to maintain a perspective of humility and kindness. You do not need to do big things in life. You do not need to find the one true love that gives life meaning. But you do not just owe it to yourself. You also owe it to your family. Even if you have a troubled relationship with your family, they will be impacted by your attitude towards life. They will be especially impacted if you choose to end it. People with depression often struggle to find meaning in their lives. They do not think anyone needs them or cares about them. This is the reason why you need to take the opportunity to find new reasons to live when you feel like you cannot go on."

"You have incredible value just for being you. You just must keep on living. You only need to start acting with kindness. It is enough to be a participant in life and contribute to others around you. Over time, this new attitude will create a groundswell of momentum in your life. You will start to naturally understand your reasons for living. You will be able to articulate them to yourself and others

around you. In the meantime, you just need to make a commitment to yourself that your life has value. You just need to make the decision that your greatest challenges can be your greatest opportunity."

"You just need to start contributing to the lives of others by acting with a little kindness. In this way, your life will slowly change, for the better. In time, you will look back at this moment as one of the most transformative and powerful moments of your life."

Lesson 3: Positive Affirmations

Affirmations work to make all aspects of your life better because they help to make your life rich with positivity. This helps you to maintain your relationships and find greater success by helping you to meet your various goals. This boosted Joy's confidence and helps her to visualise exactly where she wants to be both now and in the future. Joy finds that positive affirmation helps her stay on track with her wants and needs.

For Joy, positive affirmations work for her to help block out negativity energy from her life and as she continues with these affirmations, she notices that the negative things in her life are reduced. Even when some negative things exist, Joy begins to see them in a more positive light. In fact, you can even recite an affirmation each day to help ensure this, such as *"I abandon old habits and choose new positive ones"* or *"I choose to feed my mind more positive thoughts than negative ones, to enable my mindset to change."* Both serve to help you look past the negativity and see things in your life as a good thing, even if the only benefit is a lesson learned.

Positivity goes a long way in helping you to build a better life for yourself. Once you start your positive affirmation journey, keep track of the positive things that are happening in your life, using post-it notes.

After a couple of months, look back and you are sure to see multiple positive differences. Most people are amazed at how much a simple affirmation can do for their outlook.

When you are positive, you will also attract positive people and things, making your life a more positive experience overall with people, things and your overall home and work environment.

When you are using positive affirmations each day, you will naturally become a more optimistic person.

This means that you will start seeing the good in situations and you will be able to look ahead and see that only good things are to come. When people are more optimistic, it does a lot of good things for their health and well-being. One of the most famous health benefits is a healthier heart. Negativity and pessimism can be rather dangerous for heart health. Optimism can help to reduce your blood pressure and heart rate, ensuring a healthier heart and better overall general health.

One of the primary purposes of positive affirmations is to bring good things to your life.

Joy discovered when she repeated these daily, good things started to happen, and she noticed them more due to being a happier and more positive person. When you are happy with yourself you begin to attract positive things, people and relationships into your life. These are going to help to improve your mood and help you to see how the little things in life truly do add up. Keep track of those small things so that you can look back and reflect on them on your bad days in the future.

Life is all about perspective and you can choose how you view the people, things and situations in your life.

Positive affirmations help you to view these in a better manner so that they are a positive force in your life. You can directly use this technique to improve your perspective on a variety of things. For example, you can say something like *"I choose to see the good in life"* to boost the positivity of your general life perspective.

Having a great life focus is critical for having a good life. A lot of people do not put a lot into staying focused because they are unaware of how to do it and how it can benefit them. When you are using positive affirmations, you will be able to dictate where your focus is going to be, making it a lot easier for you to dedicate time and energy to it. For example, if you are going for a promotion, this is going to be a focus in your life. Once you make it a focus, you can take all the steps necessary to help solidify your chance to getting it. For example, if you are focussing on a promotion to become a Manager, keep telling yourself, *"I am the Manager."* Believe and act like you have already landed the job of a Manager. This will boost your confidence and allows you to see yourself where you want to be. This helps you to create specific goals and gain the motivation necessary to achieve them.

Being more grateful does a lot to ensure that you are a positive person who is attracting positive things. This happens gradually, but when you are getting what you need, you will naturally start to be more grateful for what you have and what you achieve. Positive affirmations help you to achieve your goals, giving you even more to be grateful for.

You will even notice that you start to be grateful for things, even when they do not go as you wanted them to, making you more grateful for lessons and the smaller things in life.

You can start using positive affirmation today to improve your life and help you to get started on where you want to be. Think about one thing that you want right now and make this your positive affirmation.

Here is a book on this topic that Joy enjoys:

Acts Of Faith by Iyanla Vanzant, Life Coach is a thoughtful and inspirational book that explores the unique pressures on people of colour today with great insight and sensitivity.

Each day of the year has a unique inspirational quote or message with it, along with a short essay to assist in reflection and wisdom. These messages are pulled from a great variety of spiritual practices and teachings, to assist spiritual people across faiths and disciplines. This book is invaluable for people of colour in search of motivation and support as they journey on their spiritual path.

"Application is the most important aspect of reading self-help books. There are great exercises, summaries, and thoughtful open-ended questions that will help you not only reinforce what you have learnt but apply it as well. Only when you apply is when you finally see the real physical growth and changes within you, whatever you are looking to improve on," Joy writes.

Writing Allows You To Tell A Story Nobody Wants To Hear

We live in a culture that is opposed to grief. People struggle for words and end up offering remarks or statements that belittle your grief.

Before Joy's bereavement, she admits that she too was ignorant about what to say to a grieving person.

How many times did well-meaning friends, lost for words, offer meaningless platitudes? *"He'll be okay,"* some would say, when it was clear that Aaron was never going to be okay again.

"You'll be okay," was just as hurtful. Of course Joy would be okay. She had not died, even if it felt like part of her had. But she needed people to acknowledge her grief, not diminish it. Joy wrote:

"Writing was a way of me giving voice to my story nobody wanted to hear. I needed to say the things that I could not say that even the doctors would not say, as I desperately clung on to hope."

It was only in the pages of her manuscript that Joy could safely and without judgement write this messy story in the raw voice of pain. It helped Joy understand it and slowly craft a new narrative.

Writing Allows You To Hold On To Memories

Writing was also an effective way to hold on to the memory of Joy's son.

"I documented this story as it was unfolding - the way Aaron reacted to hospital treatment; the way I reacted to the words 'palliative care' when it entered my conversation; the way Aaron looked before and after each hospital procedure; the intimate but fearful messages he texted me; the last loving words he/we spoke to each other and the way he looked at me as his strength faded during his final moments. My fondest memories of my son will be a way of holding on to the things I love and the things I never want to lose. When someone you love becomes a memory, the memory becomes a treasure," Joy wrote.

Writing Helps Find Recovery After Loss

For several years after Joy's bereavement, the story she told about herself focused on the events that had burnt her life down. It was what defined her at that moment, and she did not want it taken away from her.

Today she can tell her story as a narrative of redemption. Joy stumbled into the dark woods of grief and she came out of it transformed, stronger, and more aware of the preciousness of life. It is a story she shares with those who accept grief as an opportunity for deep transformation.

By sorting the core of her personal grief story into a narrative arch, Joy can see how personal growth results from conflict and suffering. She could finally see redemption and envision a new ending for her story.

Lescott writes: *"I do not know how I would have coped without my writing; it is what has guided me through my pain; showed me a way forward and given me a sense of hope. No matter what anybody else thinks, you know yourself best. You can devise a plan of action to help yourself rebuild your life and no one has to have input into that plan except you."*

"What is something painful you have been avoiding writing about?"

Shake The Pain Off Grief – Begin To Feel Better Again

Regaining her strength and vitality, being able to transform the pain from the loss of her son into forever memories was Joy's goal. She did not think that that was ever possible in the beginning, but little by little as she set aside time for herself, she was able to move her life forward. She was embarking on a new journey alone without her darling first born.

Someone we cared deeply about is now gone from us. We cannot hear Aaron's voice. We cannot touch him, and he is not here to help us. That is devastating. The death of a loved one can have a devastating effect on our well-being. Grief can be overwhelming and draining for months, or even years. However, we all have at our disposal an important tool to help us cope: writing.

Joy wrote, *"Writing while grieving boosted my immune system and increased my emotional and mental well-being. At first, it triggered strong emotions, like crying and feeling extremely upset for weeks and months. Writing is an instrument of self-exploration, self-expression, and self-discovery that provides you with a safe space to simply be yourself, without being judged. It is especially useful when there are things unsaid, emotions unshared, and no closure gained. The healing power of writing comes from being in a safe place to reflect on the meaning of life and death, to be relieved from shackling thoughts, and to release whatever burden you have in your chest."*

Healing Questions To Ask Yourself

When Mourning

When we go through hard times and survive to tell the tale, it is our responsibility to do so.

"I have seen the good, the bad, and the ugly. Lived it and I am still here to talk about it and help someone else if I can." - Iyanla Vanzant.

When coping with the death of a loved one the most important factor in finding peace is how you communicate with yourself. Why? Because coping with the massive changes involved when a loved one dies has little to do with what happens on the outside but everything to do with our commitment to adapt to the new circumstances we face. That is an inside job.

If we work on our inner life and realise, we have great power within, then it is possible to overcome any obstacle. This journey can be accomplished by addressing 7 key questions.

1.   **How many times have I said, *"I love you?"*** I have often said that love begins with self and recognising the mystery and power within that makes you the one and only you on this planet. You are special. Recognise that every person needs to know they are loved.

To express your love in words to the self, the deceased, and those who are close to you feeds your soul. Look for the appropriate time to write or say *"I love you"* to your loved one (you will always have a relationship with the deceased) and those who are in your family and social circle. *"I now know that nothing in my life will change until I change the way I see my life and myself."* - Iyanla Vanzant. If you want to make a change in your life, you must start with yourself. There are no pass outs, no handouts and no shortcuts. It can be uncomfortable to admit to yourself that maybe you do not like who you see when you look in the mirror but doing so opens the opportunity for the greatest gift you could ever give yourself: self-love.

2. **What is my mission now?** No one truly enjoys their life without the sense that they are contributing. Take time out to examine options for creating or continuing with a purpose or mission you previously have embraced. If you have none, consider who, how, where, or what you will devote your time and energy to in honouring your loved one. How will you keep his/her memory alive? Or perhaps carving a new way of using your talents, adding to them, or enhancing the health and spirit of yourself and others will provide new ideas for a mission.

3. **How can I be helpful to others?** The answer to this question can set your inner life on a course that brings great satisfaction, eases pain, and elevates self-esteem. It will take the focus off self by assisting in the journey of re-investing in life. The world is full of people who need your presence and caring. That same presence and caring will come back into your grief work from others. What you give out is what you receive.

4. **What do I want?** This is a question we all must ask ourselves periodically throughout life for one simple reason: it helps us create goals and evaluate our values. Without clearly written goals, which we use as a reminder, we are at the mercy of time, forgetfulness, and the influence of others.

5. **How can you best promote health and well-being for your whole body and mind at the deepest level possible?** Because of your terrible grief and loss happening, probably one of the most difficult challenges you will face will be to determine how to best promote health and wholeness to your body and mind at the deepest level possible. Because of the uniqueness of your personal grief happening there is not one cure-all formula. Perhaps you are uncertain how to proceed. Maybe you feel helpless and hopeless. Possibilities of ever having happiness again may appear unattainable. Yet, you have not lost all the character traits that make you. These traits make you powerful and strong.

"So many of us invest a fortune making ourselves look good to the world, yet inside we are falling apart. It's time to invest on the inside." - Iyanla Vanzant.

6.   **How can you quietly but purposely work 'under the radar' and quietly heal yourself from the inside out?** Many who have experienced shattering grief and loss quietly start on a wholesome amazing grief journey. They do it under the radar. They do it quietly but powerfully. Life begins with you. Power to heal begins with you. *"What you focus on expands."* - Oprah Winfrey. Take time to decide what your resolve will be, how you will do it, and when you will do it. Keep telling yourself you can start healing and quietly take the actions necessary to stop grieving and start healing. You can begin healing from within. You have more strength than you might have ever used before your grief experience. Search within until you find that empowerment. You can!

7.   **What actions are essential to bring you inner harmony, peace, and balance?**

After grief happens it is important to examine what if any physical and emotional conditions can or cannot be overcome. It is necessary to determine what you have the strength and energy to do to begin your healing journey. Baby steps may be all you do in the beginning. The key is - some action is necessary on your part; doing nothing will not sustain restoration of happiness and healing. *"Whatever is in me is stronger than what is out there to defeat me."* - Caroline Myss.

How The Coronavirus News 2020 Lifted My Spirits

As Joy discussed earlier in this book, mourning the death of a loved one is extremely hard, and the Coronavirus crisis adds to an even more difficult situation. The Coronavirus, also known as COVID-19, has nearly killed millions of people around the world.

In addition to the deaths pertaining to the virus, the bereaved are more than likely to be experiencing the loss of a family member or friend for other reasons, such as an accident, old age or another illness.

This is an exceedingly tough time for people who are experiencing a loss, because they have to deal with increased trauma and are not able to conduct a traditional funeral or service surrounded by people who can support them fully. Without their usual support network, and potentially quarantined alone at home, survivors can suffer even more than they would have in regular circumstances.

Today, 27th March 2020 – People are going through difficulties – they are going through uncertainty, divorce, loss of jobs, bereavement and much more. The population are already on an uncertain panorama and the Coronavirus has exaggerated it.

None of us knows when the COVID-19 pandemic will end; we do not know how it will end; and, at present, we can only speculate about its long-term political and economic impact.

As the Coronavirus lockdown brought the economy to a standstill, schools had shut down and healthcare workers scurried around to deal with a shortage of beds for the growing number of individuals infected by the virus. Numbers of infections and fatalities rose, and many people were forced into isolation. Cities and even countries shut, and many people were forced into isolation by the Government.

But surrounded by all the worrying news, there have been reasons to find hope. During the time of social distancing and high anxiety, it helped Joy to take a step back. It reminded her of ways to remain upbeat considering the devastation caused by the Coronavirus around the world.

Here is what has been keeping Joy uplifted through this difficult time without panicking:

- *"Pausing to appreciate and connect with nature was a great way to calm my mind. I was riding out the Coronavirus at home whilst studying the surroundings in my garden, observing the wildlife; listening to the sound of birds and other creatures and participated in gardening to care for the earth. A brisk 10 minute walk and a daily workout - one of the easiest ways to get more active, lose weight and become healthier counted towards me and my child's recommended weekly exercise. Within hours, neighbours in my community were also out in their front and back gardens either gardening or encouraging their children to play, dig and plant their own garden areas during the beautiful sunshine. For me, this underscored how nature can bring people together at such a frightening time. Animals are innocent creatures. While our world grinds to a halt, theirs carries on. We can learn a lot from them.*

- *With the conversations turning to the Coronavirus as it always seemed to do in the daily news – the school community where my youngest son attends mentioned in a series of text messages what they were doing at school during the virus outbreak. Even before schools around the UK shut down, my child's school clearly communicated their expectations with students around how learning would continue if the Government forced the school to close due to the Coronavirus. The school provided free school meals and food hamper supplies for entitled students. A Psychology Service was also offered to parents to raise any issue with a Psychologist around their children and family situation during the school closure due to the virus. In all the upheaval this pandemic has brought me as a parent, re-assurance by the teachers' care for the students who look up to them and rely on them.*

- *Reading posts on social media that brought a smile to my face "Remember laughing at Michael Jackson wearing masks and gloves? Now y'all out here looking like you wanna be starting something." It is fun to share a good laugh – it strengthens our immune system, lightens our burdens; inspires hope; connects us to others; keeps us grounded, focused and alert.*

- *With millions of people stuck in isolation, the abundance of my time at home has given me more time as a Writer to get creative and finalise this book. Social media users shared details of their new hobbies, including art, reading, baking, knitting and painting. While social distancing because of the virus is likely to last a while, it is evident that creative energy can still flourish amid a crisis.*

- *Going through a spiritual awakening was one of the most confusing, lonely, alienating but also beautiful experiences in life. Spiritual awakenings mark the beginning of your initiation on the spiritual path. Without experiencing one, we go through life pursuing emptiness to find true happiness. The beautiful thing about spiritual awakenings is that they occur at the least unexpected times. They come into your life and shake everything up like a tornado. But the hidden gift is that they occur at the precise time that you need them the most. Through daily meditation, I have created a clearing of calm and tranquillity that I can tap into within seconds whenever I feel the need. Since starting my meditation habit, my brain has literally been rewired for happiness, peace and success. The benefits of meditation are endless - reduces stress; increases your sense of well-being; increases your sense of connectedness and empathy; improves focus; improves relationships; makes you more creative; improves memory; improves your ability to make decisions; improves cardiovascular health; enhances your immune system; reduces physical and emotional pain and takes you towards enlightenment. Get meditating!*

- *A familiar sound filled the stale semi-silence of my new work-from-home reality. We were all cooped up. We were self-isolated, and we felt that way too. Listening and jamming to my favourite soothing music mixes during the outbreak downtime provided me with energy to unwind my mind and calm my soul. I sang and danced around my living room for self-love, tapping my feet to energetic beats. Music and dance is like my therapy; it serves as a medium for my physical, mental, emotional and social development and release. This was also happening in my corner of social media too, as some of my friends took to live-streaming on Facebook – doing something they were passionate about and keeping the positive musical vibes spreading across the social media community. Between a hectic work and home life it was often easy to feel disconnected from those around me. As the virus affected us all, it brought many communities around the world together. In Italy, where a countrywide lockdown took place, people joined together on their balconies for morale-boosting songs.*

- *Learning how a mother explained to her baby girl, just 5 years old how serious the Coronavirus was, she immediately began to pray. One of the things this little girl asked God to do was "let the Coronavirus go." Out of the mouths of babes (and suckling) is said when a child says something that surprises all because he/she has a wise head on young shoulders and is very sensible. So many people reached out to the mother in relation to the video that she posted on Facebook of her daughter praying to God. The mother thanked those who commented, shared, liked her daughter's prayer. Mother commented, "The love was ridiculous."*

- *BBC News shared stories of how people were helping and looking out for each other.*

- *BBC Local Radio launched a campaign called 'Make A Difference' – broadcasting stories highlighting how communities pulled together.*

- *Facebook Public Group 'Shine A Light To Fight Coronavirus' – 39,223 members was set up for anyone to get involved on 3rd April 2020 at 8:30 p.m. to unite, shine and light up the sky with a torch in their gardens for 2 minutes to remember those who unfortunately lost their lives and those fighting this terrible virus.*

- *As countries went into lockdown over the virus, there were significant drops in pollution levels and in nitrogen dioxide – a serious air pollutant and powerful warming chemical - amid reduced industrial activity and car journeys.*

- *There were plenty of stories of selfishness - panic buying and fights over toilet paper and food, but the virus also stimulated acts of kindness around the world. 2 New Yorkers gathered 1,300 volunteers in 72 hours to deliver groceries and medicine to elderly and vulnerable people in the city. Facebook reported hundreds of thousands of people in the UK had joined local support groups set up for the virus, while similar groups had been formed in Canada, creating a trend there known as 'care mongering.' Supermarkets across the country were among those who created a special 'elderly hour' so older shoppers and those with disabilities had a chance to shop in peace.*

- *During these unprecedented times of the virus, joining with my neighbours on 26th March 2020 and every Thursday evening in a big applause from our front doors to show all nurses, doctors, GPs and carers our appreciation for their on-going hard work and fight against this virus seemed the right thing to do. Neighbours in the neighbourhood lit up with some fireworks to mark the occasion.*

- *The Coronavirus affected us all in many ways: physically, emotionally, economically, socially and psychologically. All of us are (or soon will be) dealing with very real challenges of widespread serious illness and the inabilities of healthcare systems to cope with it, social and community disruption and financial problems … and the list goes on.*

When we are facing a crisis like this, fear and anxiety are natural responses to challenging situations mixed with danger and uncertainty. It is easy to get lost in worrying about all sorts of things that are out of our control: what might happen in the future; how the virus might affect us and our loved ones; how the virus will affect our financial stability or our jobs – and so on. The more we focus on what is not in our control, the more hopeless or anxious we are likely to feel. The most useful thing anyone can do in any crisis whether it be Coronavirus related or otherwise, is to focus on what is in your control.

We cannot control what happens in the future – only Jehovah God can. Maybe we all need to open our eyes, wake up and realise what is really going on around us in the world today. Have you ever thought that maybe there is a possibility the world may be experiencing a 'world awakening'? Has it crossed your mind that maybe you need to take this time of isolation from the distractions of the world to have a personal relationship with yourself where you focus on the ONLY thing in the world that really matters, the creator – Jehovah God?

We cannot control Coronavirus itself or how the Government manages this awakening situation. We cannot magically control our feelings of fear and anxiety. But we can control what we do here and now, because what we do from here and now can make a huge difference to us and our loved ones.

Everyone can do their part to protect themselves and help the Government respond to this emerging public health threat, which can result in death. We can make a big difference to the community and world around us if we just learn to **stop, listen, act, be obedient, show love and have respect** *for Government's guidance on social distancing for everyone in the UK, including children, young people and those vulnerable groups who are at increased risk of severe illness from the virus. These procedures advise us on social distancing measures we all should be taking seriously and following to reduce social interaction between people in order to reduce the transmission of the Coronavirus. We can spread good basic hand-washing and respiratory hygiene practices by being respectful and considerate to others.*

L O C K D O W N is a time to:

L – isten to God's voice and reflect. Let go and let God.
O – bey God's word and his teachings.
C – all on Jesus' name and be calm.
K – now what is the purpose of all of this.
D – well in God's presence. Do not panic and have faith.
O – ffer a prayer for everyone's safety.
W – ait and be patient. This too shall pass.
N – urture our personal relationship with ourselves and God.

"Jehovah God, please help China and the rest of the world overcome this current pandemic when you see fit. This contagion has demonstrated that the Chinese Government needs to learn lessons from the current situation and reflect on how it has affected your beautiful creation; the country's well-being and mortality from the COVID-19 virus." Amen.

In this time, it is important for us to remember that money is not everything - that it is the health of people around the world that is most important. As humans, we have to overcome this issue together in unity. It is time to stand with each other, rather than be separated by fear, greed and hostility."

"We all are so deeply interconnected; we have no option but to love all.

Be kind and do good for anyone, and that will be reflected.

The ripples of the kind heart are the highest blessings of the Universe. Only connect."

One day you too will tell your own story of how you have overcome what you are going through right now, and it will become part of someone else's survival guide.

Poem: Death Is Nothing At All

"*Death is nothing at all.*

I have only slipped away into the next room.

Whatever we were to each other we still are.

Call me by my old familiar name.

Laugh as we always did; at the little jokes we enjoyed together.

Pray, smile and think of me.

Life means all that it ever meant.

It is the same as it ever was.

There is unbroken continuity.

Why should I be out of mind because I am out of sight?

My spirit is floating high above.

Roaming, watching those I deeply love.

Weeping faces I do not want to see.

Smile be happy when you remember me.

I am waiting to be with you soon."

ABOUT THE AUTHOR

Joy Lescott is the courageous author, of *'Happy To Help' – A Mother's Biography Of Aaron Jeffers.*

Her first ever memoir is derived from the earth-shattering pain of losing a loved one, her 23- year-old son, the deceased, 6 years ago which left her heartbroken.

She does her best writing with passion and truth, from her heart – fuelled by pain; entering into her deep hurts, scars and wounds to allow her to process them in her own unique, creative and rewarding way only to find both healing and beautiful things taking place: not by avoiding discomfort, but by honestly leaning on it.

Breaking out of isolation and sharing the painful parts of her story is about more than just Joy. It is about Joy encouraging others to reveal parts of themselves they would rather hide. Other people may identify with certain pieces of her pain, and in Joy's story find healing. Her purpose is to reach out to people going through the same cathartic process others have experienced, and in doing so, bring mankind a little closer.

UK-based author, Joy, is survived by her grandson.

She spends her time raising her younger son and devotes a set amount of time developing herself spiritually to improve her life and interaction with others. Joy enjoys leading a healthy lifestyle, combined with physical exercise to help promote her overall health.

In addition to writing, Joy is a Gardener who does not just love to connect with nature, the outdoors and plants, but her love of nature extends to all living things – birds, bees and butterflies delight her. Simply seeing greenery and nature helps Joy feel more relaxed, calm and keeps her grounded. By nature, she is a warm and caring individual. Joy is also an E-ACT School Ambassador who enjoys meeting new people, and gets involved in exciting projects, assisting the school's Leadership Teams to deliver their organisational strategy; celebrate students' achievements and celebrate the work of the school academies.

Printed in Great Britain
by Amazon